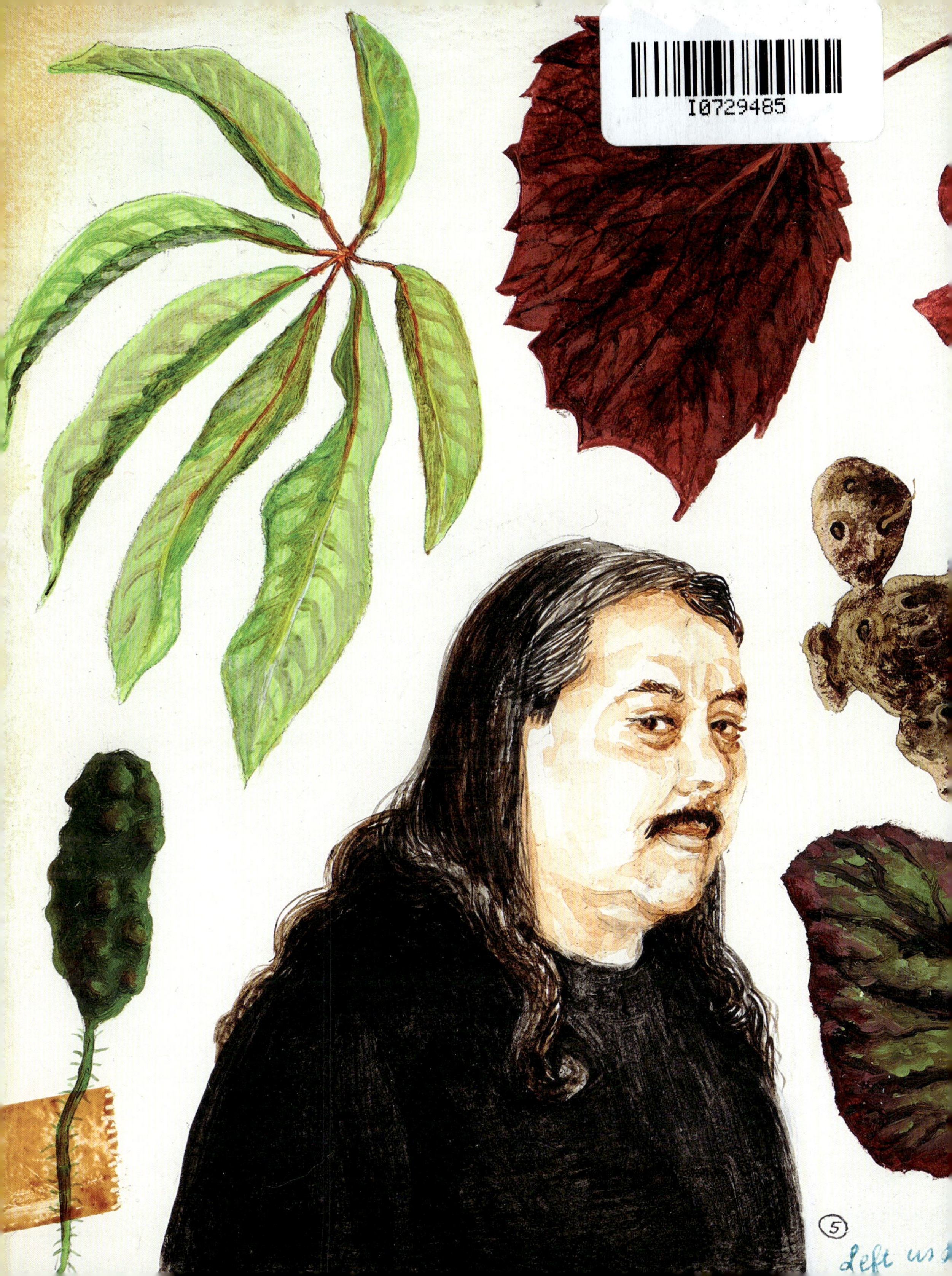

I0729485
⑤
left us

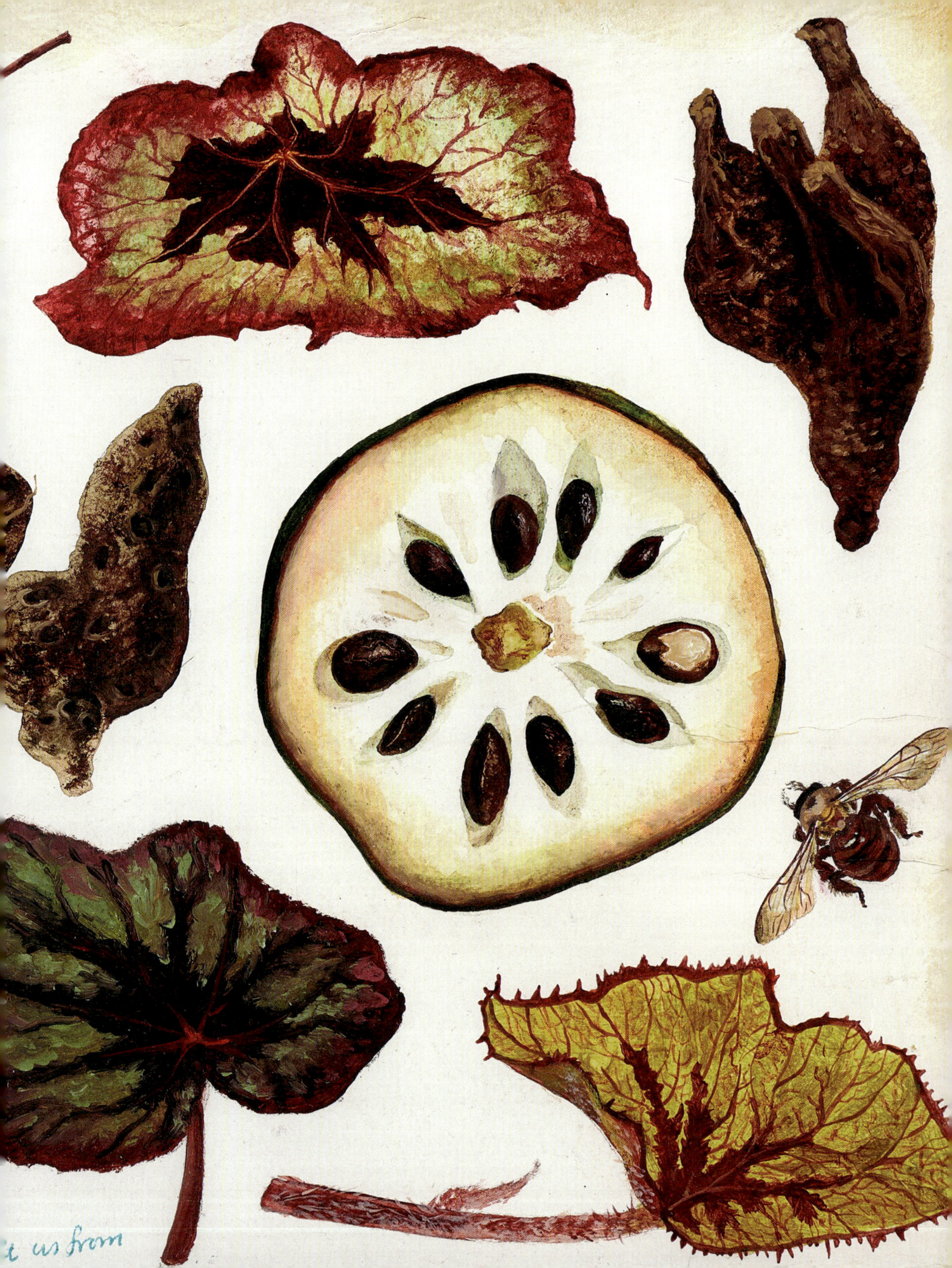
t us from

Spirit in the Land

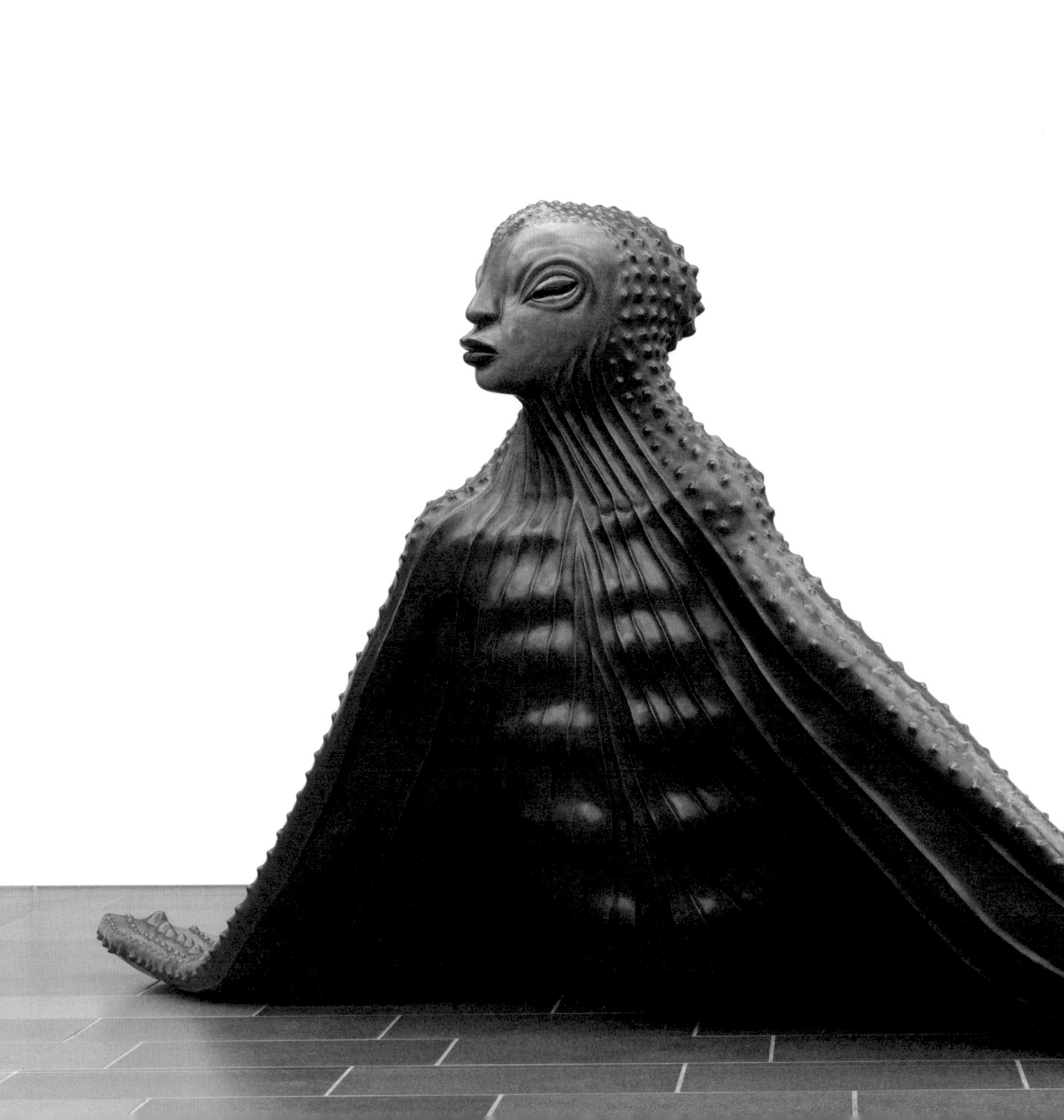

Spirit in the Land

EDITED BY TREVOR SCHOONMAKER,
MARY D.B.T. AND JAMES H. SEMANS DIRECTOR,
NASHER MUSEUM OF ART AT DUKE UNIVERSITY

PUBLISHED BY THE NASHER MUSEUM OF ART
AT DUKE UNIVERSITY

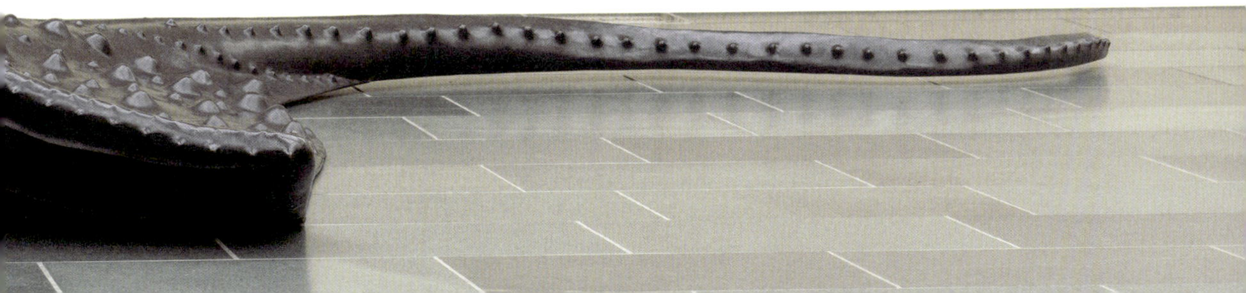

Published on the occasion of the exhibition *Spirit in the Land*, organized by the Nasher Museum of Art at Duke University, Durham, North Carolina, and curated by Trevor Schoonmaker, Mary D.B.T. and James H. Semans Director

Nasher Museum of Art
at Duke University
2001 Campus Drive
Durham, North Carolina, 27705
(919) 684-5135
www.nasher.duke.edu

Cataloging information for this title is available from the Library of Congress. Library of Congress Control Number: 2022944760
ISBN 978-0-938989-45-5

Distributed by Duke University Press

Edited by Trevor Schoonmaker

Design and typesetting:
Julie Klugman Braude

Project management: Melissa Gwynn

Copyediting: Jessica Lott

Proofreading: Molly Boarati

Set in Acumin

Color separations and printing by Puritan, Hollis, New Hampshire

Binding by Superior, Braintree, Massachusetts

Lead support for *Spirit in the Land* is provided by the Ford Foundation.

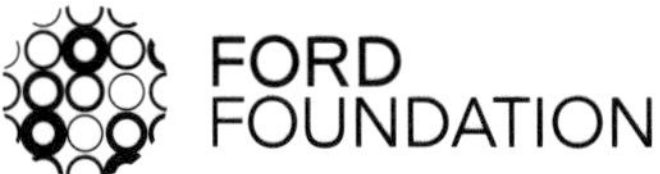

Major support for *Spirit in the Land* is provided by The Andy Warhol Foundation for the Visual Arts.

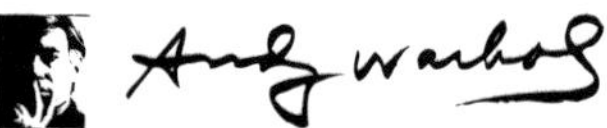

The Andy Warhol Foundation for the Visual Arts

This project is supported in part by the National Endowment for the Arts.

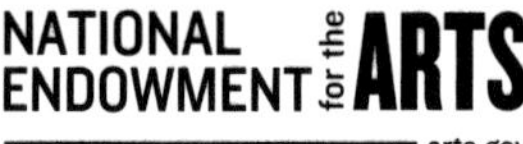

arts.gov

At the Nasher, *Spirit in the Land* is supported by The Duke Endowment; the Nancy A. Nasher and David J. Haemisegger Family Fund for Exhibitions; the Frank Edward Hanscom Endowment Fund; the Janine and J. Tomilson Hill Family Fund; Katie Thorpe Kerr and Terrance I. R. Kerr; Alexandria and Kevin Marchetti; Parker & Otis; Lisa Lowenthal Pruzan and Jonathan Pruzan; and Caroline and Arthur Rogers.

Previous page:

WANGECHI MUTU, *MamaRay*, 2020. Bronze, edition 1/3, 65 x 144 x 192 inches (165.1 x 365.8 x 487.7 cm). Commissioned by and collection of the Nasher Museum of Art at Duke University, Durham, North Carolina. Gift of Mike and Joan Kahn in honor of Douglas and Stefanie Kahn, 2020.18.1. © Wangechi Mutu. Photo by Brian Quinby.

Front cover:

HEW LOCKE, *Mosquito Hall*, 2013. Acrylic on chromogenic print, 83 7/8 x 49 3/4 inches (213 x 126.4 cm). Collection of the Nasher Museum of Art at Duke University, Durham, North Carolina. Museum purchase, 2022.22.1. © Hew Locke. All Rights Reserved, DACS 2023. Courtesy of the artist, Hales Gallery, and P•P•O•W.

Back cover:

MONIQUE VERDIN, *Tree of Life*, 2000. Inkjet print on paper, 18 x 12 inches (45.7 x 30.5 cm). Courtesy of the artist. © Monique Verdin.

Front and end papers:

RENÉE STOUT, *Botanical Illustration #3 (The Herbmaster, James Luna)* (details), 2020. Oil, acrylic, and mixed media on handmade paper; 12 5/16 x 11 13/16 inches (31.3 x 30 cm). Collection of the Nasher Museum of Art at Duke University, Durham, North Carolina. Museum purchase, 2021.23.1. © Renée Stout.

Contents

8   Preface

10   Acknowledgments

13   *Spirit in the Land*, Trevor Schoonmaker

17   Terry Adkins
19   Firelei Báez
21   Radcliffe Bailey
25   Rina Banerjee
27   Christi Belcourt
29   María Berrío
33   Mel Chin
37   Andrea Chung
41   Sonya Clark
45   Annalee Davis
48   Tamika Galanis
53   Allison Janae Hamilton
57   Barkley L. Hendricks
63   Alexa Kleinbard
67   Hung Liu
69   Hew Locke
73   Meryl McMaster
77   Wangechi Mutu
81   Maia Cruz Palileo
85   Dario Robleto
89   Jim Roche
93   Kathleen Ryan
95   Sheldon Scott
97   Renée Stout
101   Monique Verdin
105   Stacy Lynn Waddell
109   Charmaine Watkiss
113   Marie Watt
115   Carrie Mae Weems
117   Peter Williams

122   Exhibition Checklist

130   Lenders to the Exhibition

131   Nasher Museum Staff and Board Members

Preface

I began thinking about *Spirit in the Land* in 2018, shortly after
having organized two previous exhibitions that explored the
intersection of cultural and natural landscapes. In 2017, I curated
the New Orleans Triennial *Prospect.4: The Lotus in Spite of
the Swamp*, and in 2016, I co-curated *Southern Accent: Seeking
the American South in Contemporary Art* with Miranda Lash.
Researching aspects of those two projects brought me back to
my childhood experiences in nature.

Growing up in North Carolina, a state with an extraordinary range
of biodiversity from the Appalachian Mountains to the barrier
islands, I was shaped by the natural world around me—its land,
water, flora, fauna, and spirit. As a boy I spent a great deal of
my time outdoors, tending to summer squash and tomatoes in
the garden, snapping peas and shucking corn, eating wild
blackberries and scuppernong grapes, sipping on honeysuckle
and making tea from sassafras roots. Our backyard led to dense
woods with white oaks, red maples, sweetgum, tulip poplars,
loblolly pines, flowering dogwoods, eastern redbuds, and rhodo-
dendron. The forest offered endless opportunities for exploration
of its climbing trees, vernal pools, and winding creeks, observing
salamanders, frogs, crayfish, fish, turtles, snakes, birds, mantis,
and beetles…and most anything my friends and I could catch and
put in a bucket for a closer look.

Our family lived in the Western Piedmont, or foothills of Winston-
Salem, but made numerous visits each year to the coast, east
of Cape Fear and not far from the Green Swamp, the only place
in the world where the Venus flytrap grows in the wild. I spent
countless hours there fishing, crabbing, and swimming in the
ocean, salt marshes, and estuaries. The marsh provided a limitless
source of fascination, and I explored its canals and tidal creeks
whenever possible. It is a transitional space, defined more by
water or by land depending on the changing tides, with a brackish
blend of both salt and fresh water that supports an incredible
spectrum of wildlife within. Such places are a vital nursery and

home for numerous fish, crustaceans, mollusks, birds, and more. At high tide it can be relatively easily navigated by boat or kayak, when wading birds tend to their nests but dolphins come inland to feed, pelicans dive, and one might even catch a fleeting glimpse of a green turtle or diamondback terrapin. Low tide offers a dizzying array of activity and sounds, as fiddler crabs emerge from their underground lairs, mullet school and jump, and shrimp make the water vibrate as they try to elude the blue crabs, great blue herons, clapper rails, and stingrays that come to the shallows to feed. Flounder lie in wait while osprey soar overhead and kingfishers dart in and out for a quick bite. In the evening, as the sun sets, the ibises, terns, and gulls fly home to their nesting grounds. The earth here is mostly a soft, deep mud that only the lightest of animals can walk on. While not suitable for heavy humans, it provides a tremendous service by storing carbon within its thick layers of muck, while the oysters and spartina cordgrass do their part to filter out pollutants and toxins from the water. The salt marsh is a wondrous refuge of ecological efficiency, beauty, and biodiversity, but also a remote biome that is largely inaccessible and often misunderstood. It is a place of constant change and adaptation where periwinkle snails move up and down the grass as the tides rise and fall. It is a realm that repeatedly calls me back, shaping my sense of identity, curiosity, and reciprocity while restoring the spirit.

Spirit in the Land is an exhibition about finding oneself in nature and identifying as part of that ecosystem. The artists help us see not only the ways in which we humans are harming the planet, but also the ways the natural world protects, nourishes, and provides for us; they make cultural connections that help strengthen our bonds with the land, water, and life around us. As seen through the eyes of artists, nature is our teacher, and the artists are our environmental guides, our interpreters and stewards. It is through their personal perspectives and culturally diverse voices, their works and their texts, that we may reconnect with and remember to give back to the Earth.

Acknowledgments

I extend my deepest gratitude to each of the artists for their inspiring art, their vision, feedback, and encouragement, and for taking the time to compose something personal for this catalogue. Thank you for your voices, your texts, and your works!

In addition to the many lenders, I also acknowledge the following for their assistance in securing loans for the exhibition and texts for the catalogue: Marianne Boesky Gallery; James Cohan; CONNERSMITH; Paula Cooper Gallery; Eric Firestone Gallery; Ford Foundation Gallery; Gladstone Gallery; Hales Gallery; Hemphill Fine Arts; Susan Hendricks; Susan and Michael Hershfield; Nancy Hoffman Gallery; Indigenous Art Collection, Crown-Indigenous Relations and Northern Affairs Canada; Luis De Jesus Los Angeles; Karma; Jeff Kelley; Indra Khanna; Astrid Meek; Monique Meloche Gallery; Victoria Miro; Jennifer and Jason New; Tyler Park Presents; Jack Shainman Gallery; MARC STRAUS; Tia Collection; Tiwani Contemporary; Líza Williams; and Merele Williams-Adkins. I am also grateful to Julie Klugman Braude for her elegant catalogue design, Jessica Lott for her expert copyediting, Molly Boarati for proofreading, and Alexa Dilworth for her mindreading and magic with words.

At the Nasher I must thank the entire staff for their work on this exhibition, with a special mention to the following individuals: Adria Gunter, Julianne Miao, and Amanda Zarate for their organizational assistance; Marshall Price for his curatorial leadership; Wendy Hower and team for their marketing prowess; Julia McHugh and the academic initiatives team for their commitment to faculty and student engagement; Liz Peters and Ruth Caccavale for leading our tours and educational programs; Rob Knebel and team for their staffing and budgetary guidance; and Stephanie Wheatley, Amanda Koelling, and the development team for their powerful fundraising

and stewardship. I extend gratitude to Associate Registrar
Lee Nisbet for her diligent coordination of the many loans for
the exhibition, as well as Exhibition Designer Brad Johnson
and his team of Alan Dippy and Patrick Krivacka for their intuitive
understanding of each artwork and their inspired installation.
Lastly, I must express extensive thanks to our Exhibitions
and Publications Manager Melissa Gwynn, who brilliantly kept
this complex project on course with tremendous grace and
skill, even standing in as the exhibition's curatorial associate while
we were particularly short staffed. I am very grateful to work
with such a dedicated and creative team.

I would also like to acknowledge some of the environmentalists
and naturalists whose work has inspired and guided me: Rachel
Carson, whose book *The Sea Around Us* I loved as a teenager and
led me to her mighty *Silent Spring*; David Attenborough, whose
wondrous documentaries have transfixed my entire family; Robin
Wall Kimmerer, for the life guide and love poem that is *Braiding
Sweetgrass*; Tom Earnhardt for his deeply engaging and informative
PBS series, *Exploring North Carolina*; and Wangari Maathai for
leading by example through her Green Belt Movement.

Finally, I am eternally thankful for my family—my mother, Meyressa
Schoonmaker; my late father, Donald Schoonmaker; my wife,
Teka Selman; and our two daughters, Zadie and Lena—for their
love and unwavering support, and for sharing with me a genuine
sense of awe within nature. To experience that curiosity and
passion together as a family is a very gratifying thing. I would like
to dedicate this catalogue to Zadie and Lena, who at their young
ages are already great stewards of the natural world.

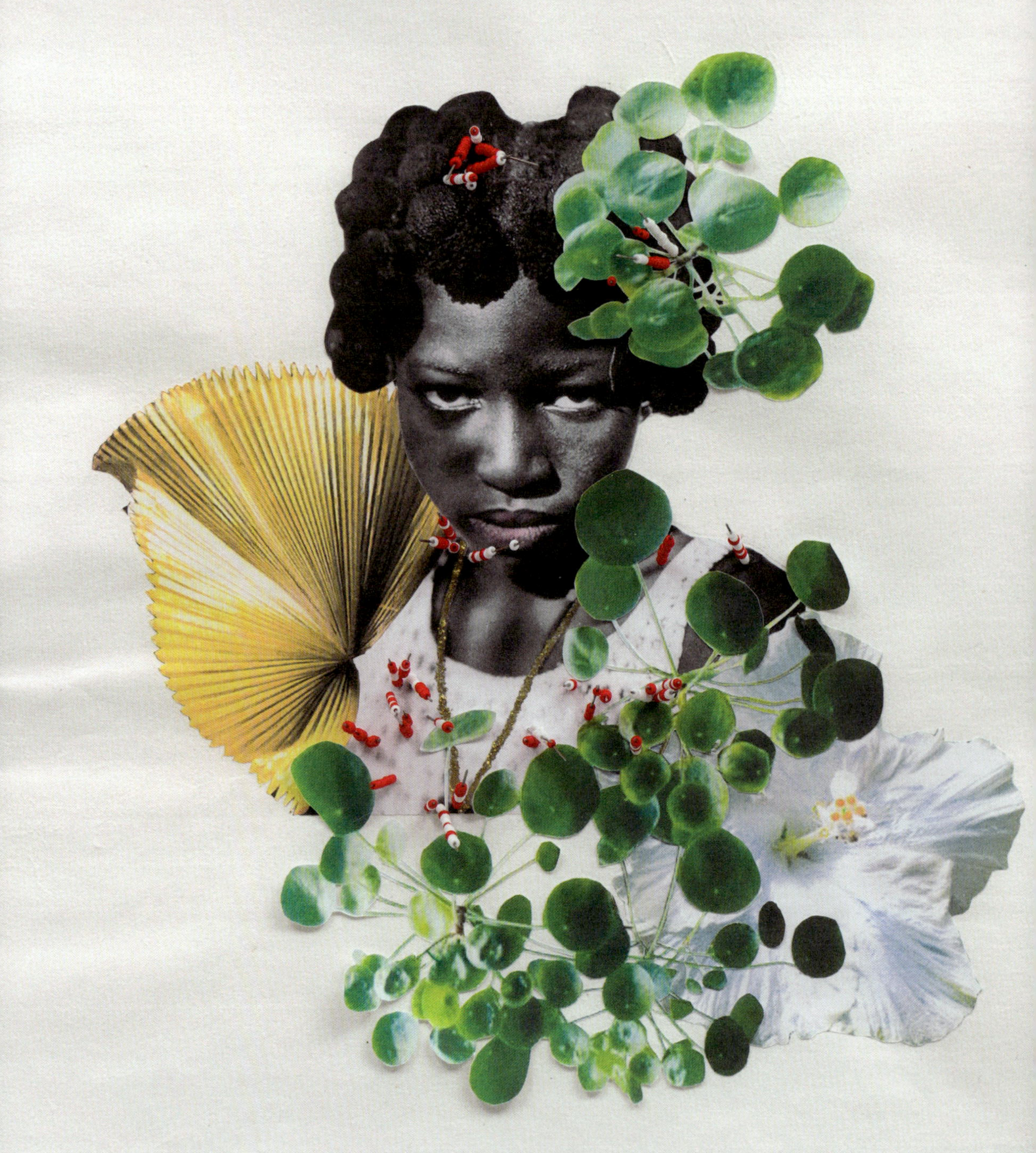

Spirit in the Land

TREVOR SCHOONMAKER

Spirit in the Land is a contemporary art exhibition that examines today's urgent ecological concerns from a cultural perspective, demonstrating how intricately our identities and natural environments are intertwined. Through their artwork, thirty artists show us how rooted in the earth our most cherished cultural traditions are, and how our relationship to land and water shapes us as individuals and communities. The works reflect the restorative potential of our connection to nature and exemplify how essential both biodiversity and cultural diversity are to our survival.

These artists explore the ways in which our inner spaces mirror our outer ones in works that both celebrate the profound beauty of our world and mourn its loss, and with it, vanishing histories of people and place.

As the battles against climate change are often most critical for marginalized communities—environmental justice is social and racial justice—the exhibition and catalogue center the voices of artists who approach ecological awareness through a close attention to the communities most negatively affected. Acting as environmental stewards, the artists reclaim and revitalize our understanding of nature as a repository of cultural memory, a place of sanctuary, a site of resistance, and a source of spiritual nourishment and healing. As land and water provide a sense of belonging and community, the exhibition illustrates our interdependence with all life on Earth.

Spirit in the Land has its roots in North America, with shoots reaching into the Caribbean. While these artists investigate natural environments under stress, the exhibition presents a belief in the possibility of transformation and regeneration. Our desire to live in harmony with nature is ultimately what will determine our future.

ANDREA CHUNG, *VEX IV*, 2020. Collage, ink, and beads on paper handmade from traditional birthing cloth; 22 x 16 ¹/₂ inches (55.9 x 41.9 cm). Image courtesy of the artist and Tyler Park Presents. © Andrea Chung. Photo by Michael Underwood.

Next page:

ALLISON JANAE HAMILTON, *Sisters, Wakulla County FL* (detail), 2019. Archival pigment print, edition 2/5, 24 x 36 inches (61 x 91.4 cm). Collection of the Nasher Museum of Art at Duke University, Durham, North Carolina. Museum purchase with funds provided by The Durham (NC) Chapter of The Links, Incorporated; 2021.13.2. © Allison Janae Hamilton. Courtesy of the artist and Marianne Boesky Gallery, New York and Aspen.

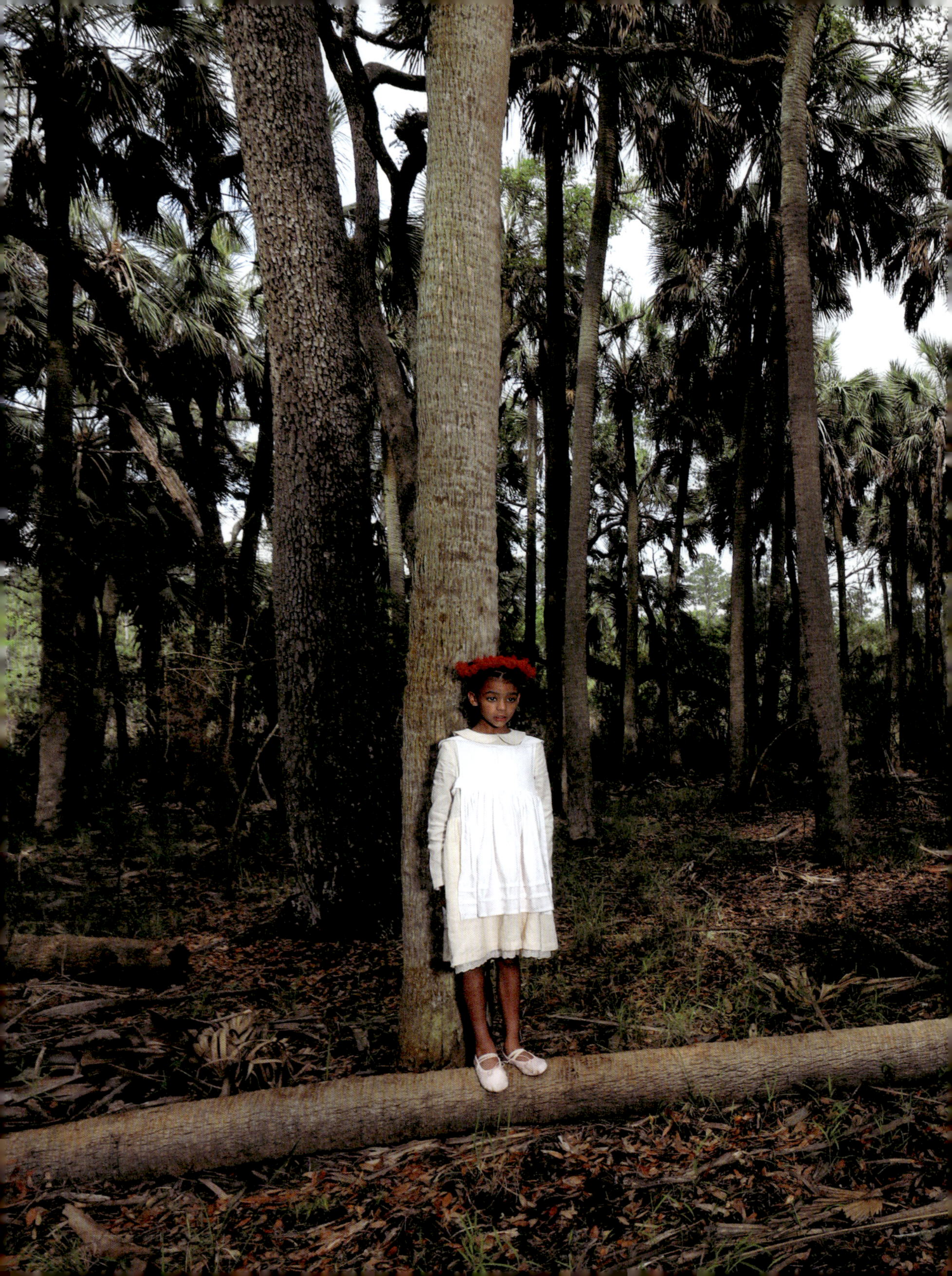

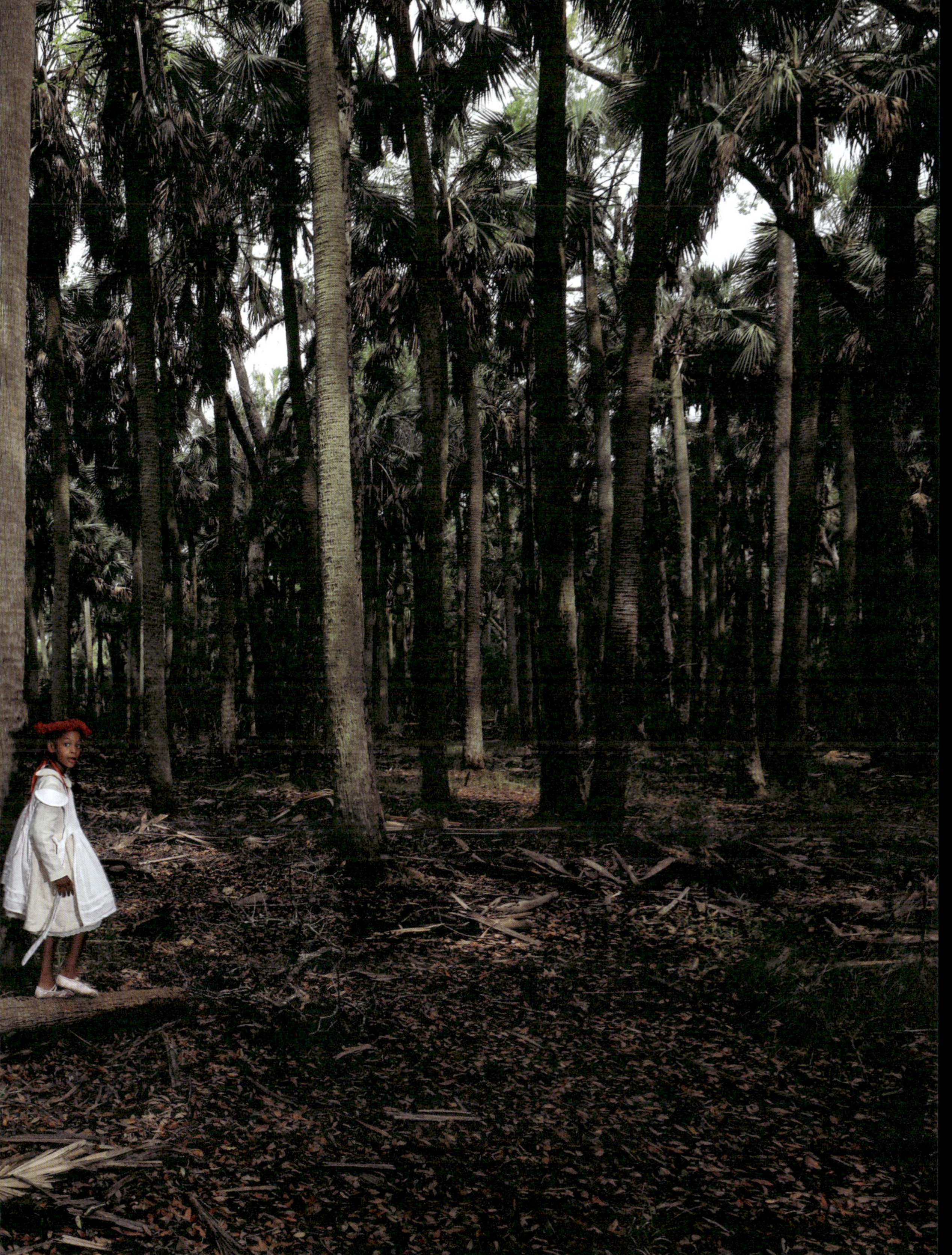

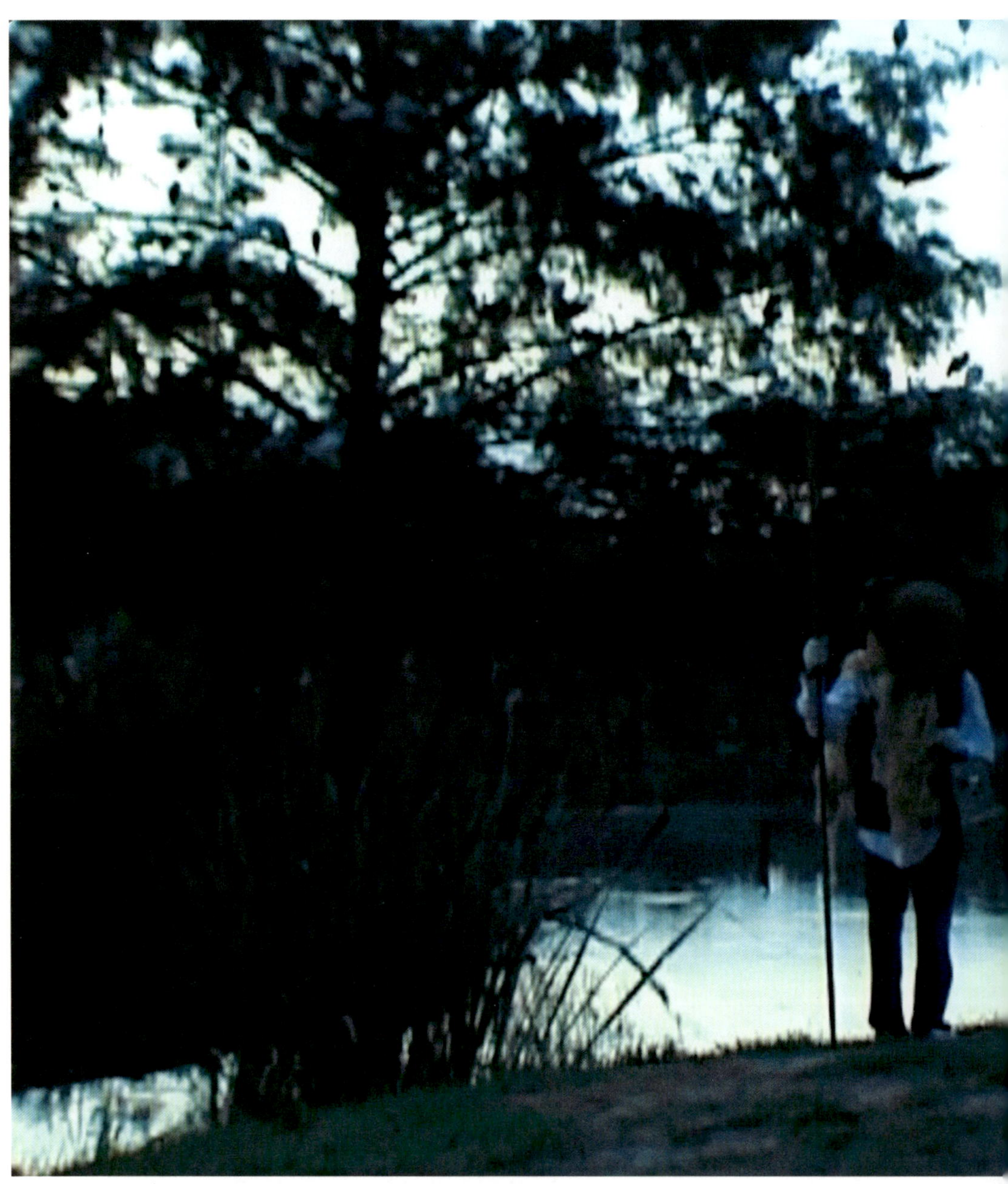

TERRY ADKINS, Still from *Roost*, 2001. Video (color, sound), 9:09 minutes. Courtesy of the artist's estate and Paula Cooper Gallery, New York. © 2022 The Estate of Terry Adkins / Artists Rights Society (ARS), New York. Courtesy Paula Cooper Gallery, New York.

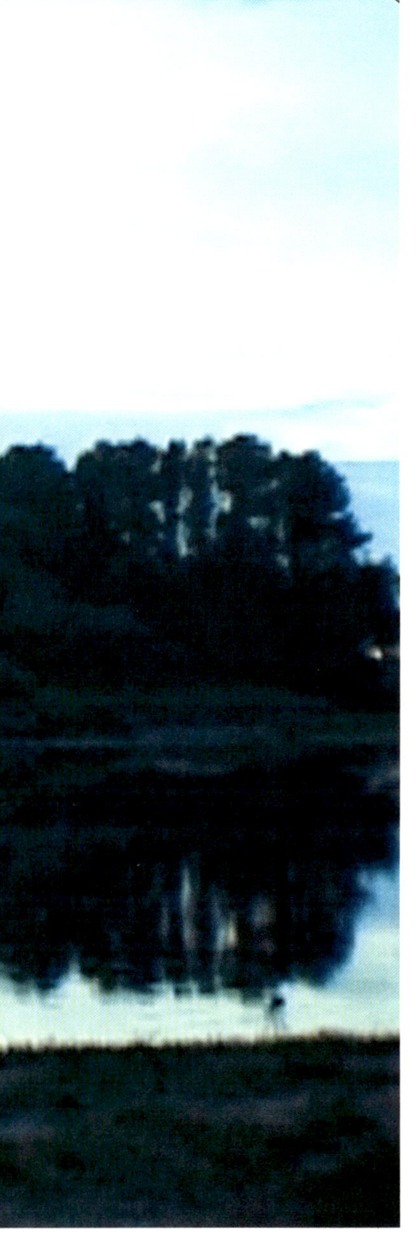

Terry Adkins

BORN IN WASHINGTON, DC, 1953; DIED 2014

This was shot in Gainesville, Florida. The human figure is represented as transcendent statuary amid the sound and movement of roosting egrets and ibises leaving the tree in the morning. The John Brown Recital traveled from Akron to Chicago to Richmond to Winston-Salem and finally to Florida. I had re-imagined that John Brown's Harpers Ferry campaign was successful and that he was able to move southward, amassing an army of fugitive slaves according to his original vision. Gainesville would have been an ideal geographical location from which to apply guerilla strategies—swampland, etc.—as well as joining forces with Seminole rebels. The appearance of basketry over the head as disguise and anonymity is a device employed by early Japanese assassins. The seeming flowing beard is made from fleece, as John Brown was also one of the foremost shepherds in America at that time, with a sheep farm in Akron. The biblical associations of the good shepherd and his flock are also intentional here. The beard is symbolic of the iconic nature of Brown's image on the American psyche and launches from the Herman Melville poem, The Portent.

> —Terry Adkins email correspondence
> with Charles Gaines, October 16, 2013.

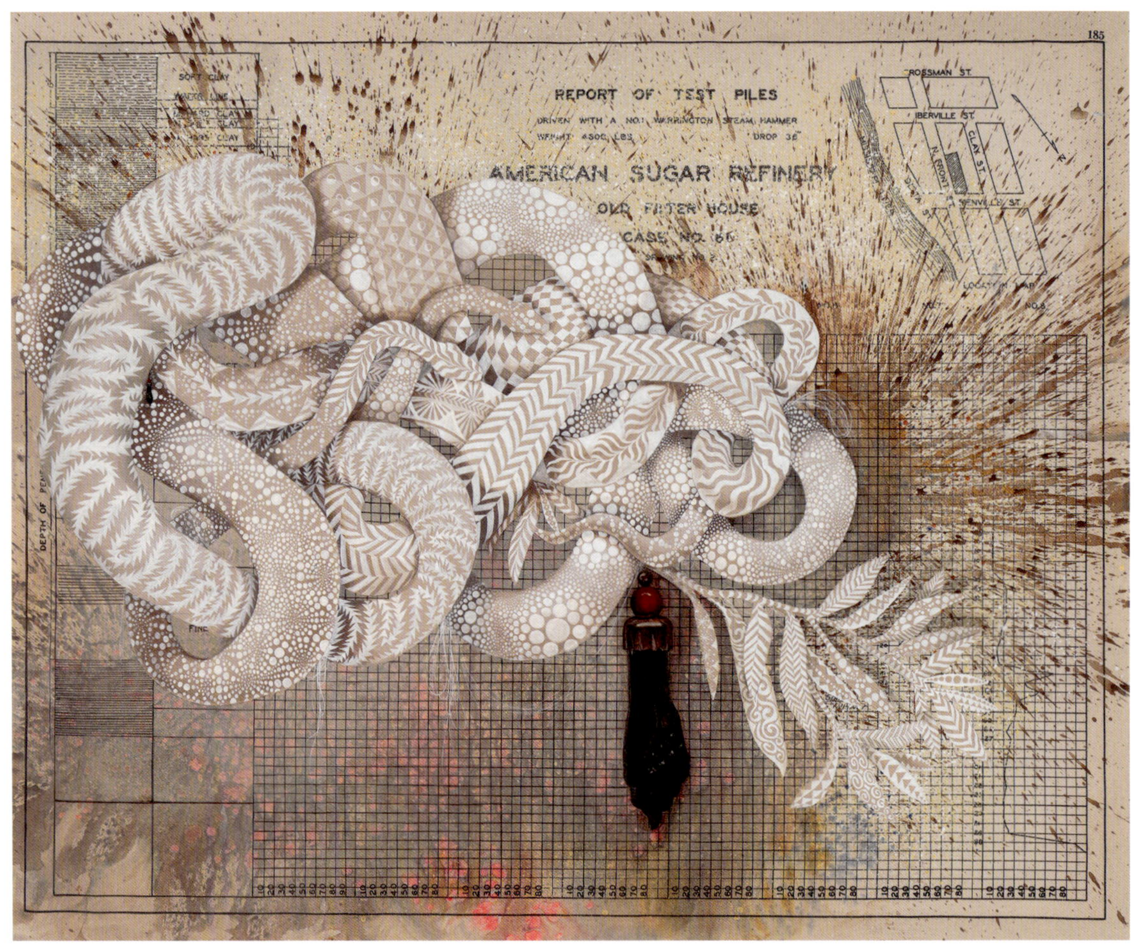

FIRELEI BÁEZ, *Tignon for Ayda Weddo (or that which a center can not hold)*, 2019. Acrylic and oil on archival printed canvas, 91 1/2 x 114 1/4 inches (232.4 x 290.2 cm). Collection of the Nasher Museum of Art at Duke University, Durham, North Carolina. Museum purchase, 2019.24.1. © Firelei Báez. Photo by Peter Paul Geoffrion.

Firelei Báez

BORN IN SANTIAGO DE LOS CABALLEROS, DOMINICAN REPUBLIC, 1981

In conversation with Trevor Schoonmaker, Nasher Museum Director

Trevor Schoonmaker: You frequently incorporate foliage or trees into your work, including in *Tignon for Ayda Weddo (or that which a center can not hold).* What role does flora play in your paintings?

Firelei Báez: For me, foliage, trees, and plant life stand in for a liminal space of embodied knowledge. They are markers of the space that both separates and binds one and another. In my work, this most often manifests as beings pictured in and within nature.

TS: *Tignon for Ayda Weddo* also includes a serpent as Haitian Loa. How do you see (or manifest) the connection between the natural and the spiritual worlds?

FB: Within this pantheon, the serpent stands for all that is beyond our conception. It holds space to be label-less, every gender, and truly full.

TS: The background in *Tignon for Ayda Weddo* is an architectural plan for a sugar refinery in New Orleans; the foundation of the painting is situated on the land where sugarcane was grown and reaped, originally by enslaved African laborers. How would you describe the importance of land itself in this painting and other works of yours?

FB: Land is, for me, a site of reciprocal influence. The mechanization of land through enslaved labor, at the cost or displacement of local flora and peoples, created the indelible bodily, psychic, and environmental scars that we can no longer look away from. The overpainting of *Ayda Weddo* is a visualization of the symbols of resistance to the trauma and violence caused by the activities of the American Sugar Refining Company, and a gesture towards decentering the acquisitive economic model that created those conditions to begin with.

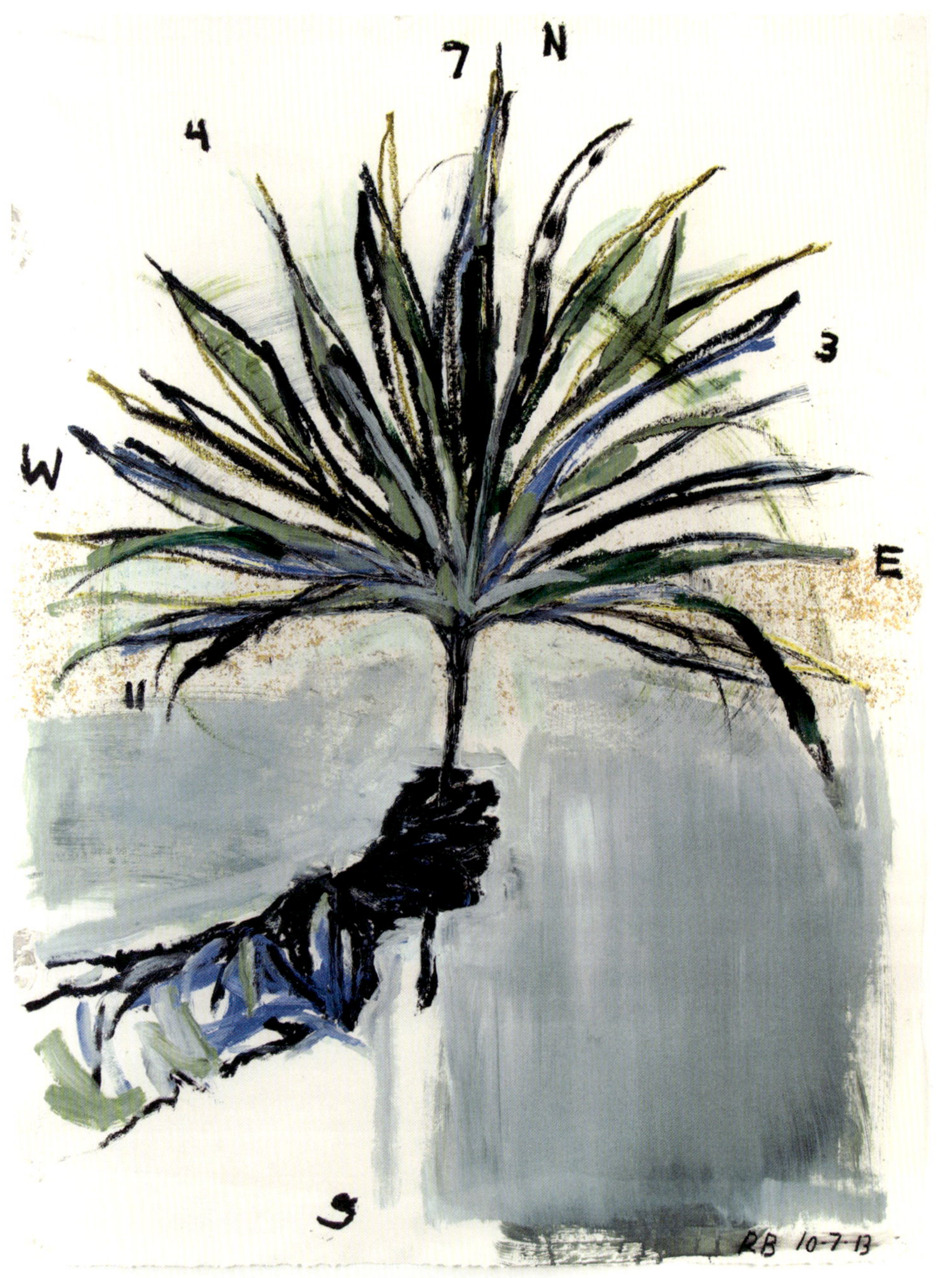
7
N
4
3
W
E
11
S
RB 10-7-13

Radcliffe Bailey

BORN IN BRIDGETON, NEW JERSEY, 1968

In conversation with Trevor Schoonmaker, Nasher Museum Director

Trevor Schoonmaker: Could you describe the land that you live on, and the natural environment that your home is nestled into? How does that inform your work?

Radcliffe Bailey: The land where I live in Atlanta backs up to a nature preserve around Utoy Creek, which is a former Civil War battleground. I believe that the region's narrative is held in the Georgia Red Clay.

TS: Is the black king snake one you see on your land? What cultural traditions are you referencing with the snake in your work? Is it made of materials that have significant importance to you?

RB: The snake is representative of the black king snakes that I see on my property. Crossing me and me crossing them. King snakes eat other snakes, so they are dominant in the food chain. The snake also represents the trails that flow throughout the property. Little trails here and there are reflective of the same movement that the snake takes. The snake is used in multiple cultures as a representative of healing and movement. Blues musicians have referenced the black king snake as a symbol in their music, especially Lightnin' Hopkins, who talked about himself as a snake in his song, "I'm a Crawling Black Snake." My snake sculpture is made out of railroad spikes. My father is a railroad engineer, and I frequently incorporate materials into my work that represent my family history.

RADCLIFFE BAILEY, *Palm*, 2013. Mixed media on paper, 64 x 50 7/8 inches (162.6 x 129.2 cm). Collection of Susan and Michael Hershfield. © Radcliffe Bailey. Courtesy of the artist and Jack Shainman Gallery, New York.

TS: The palmetto grows along the southeastern coastline, more or less following the Gullah Geechee Corridor…and it's the symbol of South Carolina. Is your work referencing the history of that land and its people? Does it specifically reference Charleston's history as a port in the slave trade, built on the skilled labor of enslaved Africans?

RB: The palm reflects those who were enslaved, as well as the palm's growth in the coastal areas of West Africa and on the islands of the Caribbean. The use of the palm also references the coasts of the Carolinas and historical churches like Mother Emanuel AME, which are located there. As to my reference of the enslaved, they were torn from their homes and sent to ports throughout the coastal areas of Africa and the islands, then brought to the ports of Charleston. The numbers address their numbers and the direction of their movement.

TS: Are the signs and numbers also a spiritual navigational chart of sorts?

RB: All of the different types of numbers used in my work are references to my own personal symbols, such as when to stop a work, the layers of thought within the work, directions, certain times of day, and birth dates.

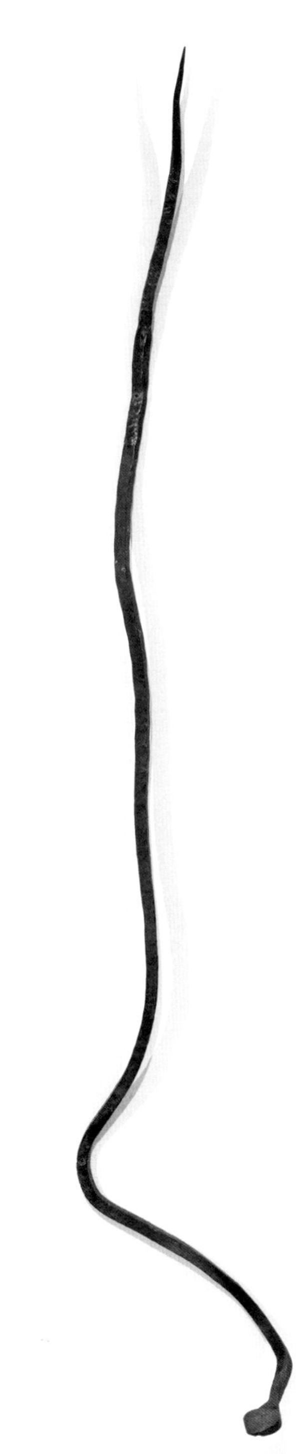

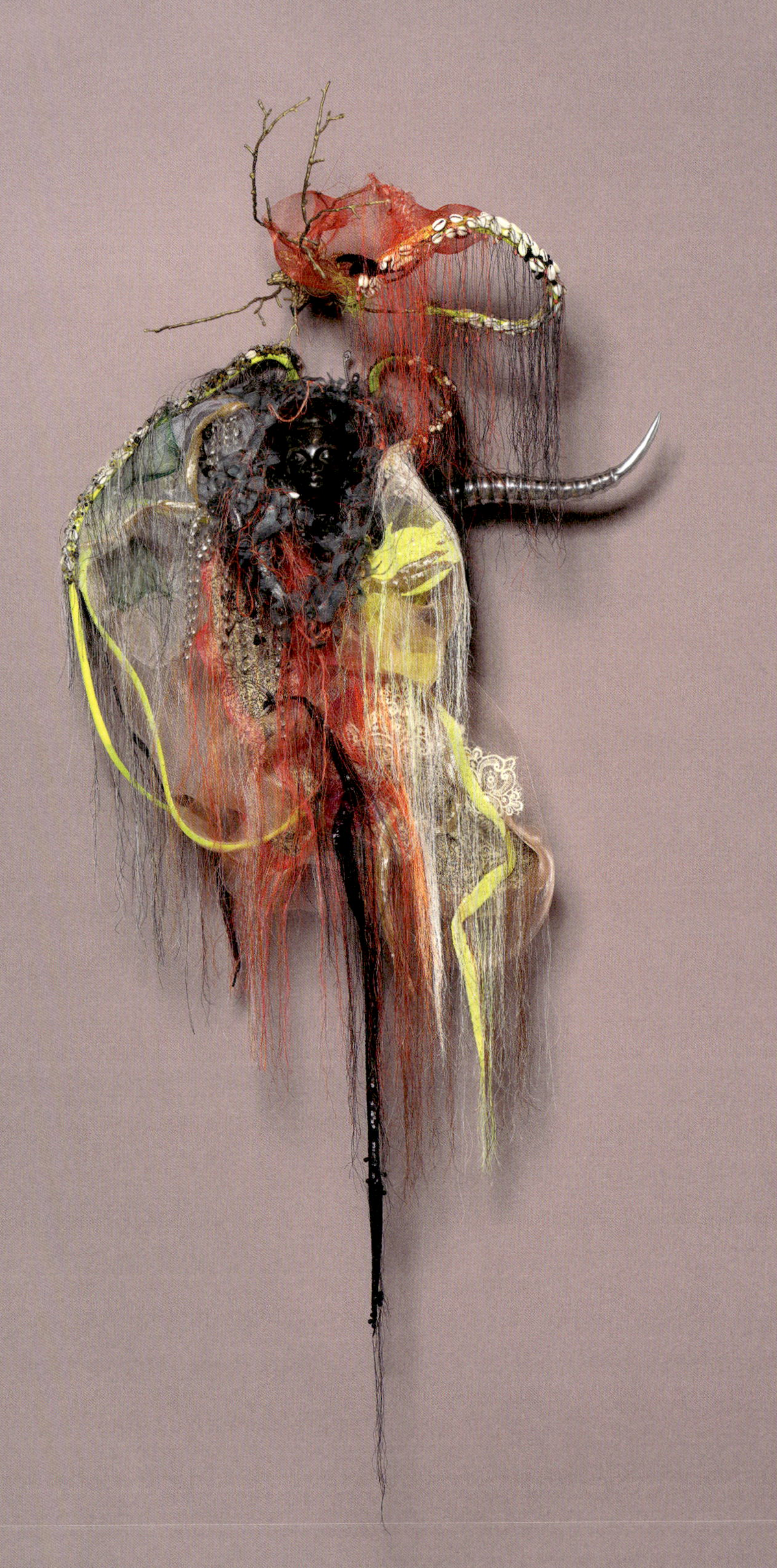

Rina Banerjee

BORN IN KOLKATA, INDIA, 1963

I am queen of the underworld, this other spirt unearthed, killed and killed again, shared and swallowed, exposed, violent, and violated. I am concentrated in spirited browns, earthy with wet blood and bosom. Remember, equality is in every soul, every silent foe in unweighted gold, it grows to glow. Find me if this possible other, in cracks between doors to unearth if you can speak slightly in angles, narrow if tight, then sit honestly beside me and believe in my light, my sight, my spirited land. Who has suffered more than I, who turn to colors shallow? Give me a reason to play alongside you who is poor of heart and spirit, and shall I follow you? Take me out with my pitch-black eyes and everything you want from me that is not whitened which can yellow, brown turn so to make me into mountains that blind sun make me Medusa's medicine, make me earth that rattles without quiet, without your strength so you may show eventually taller but see this do not make me into man as he is done.

There is no other rain cloud that has silenced so many people than that which we term patriarchy, plainly dissecting race, as this other inspirited place buried in land as would a grave of unworthy seed. The plain quality of a thousand years and more that has grounded all continents and walks of life is seen as plain and clear like daylight is a lie. The most vivid man glittering in crown waited for his chocolate cake, ginger and molasses, and his cream-curdled milk…so don't you close your eyes now when you have been sleeping in salt. We others wake together as farmed animals do into voice of tears and browned pennies stricken, bowed heads for centuries sloped towards river's edge to be drowned.

How could I take this end as female slave as gardened indignity ashamed that you cloud me, pain me, and you who will wilt to find your foe very much alive and living in spirited land.

RINA BANERJEE, *Summer squash and rice liquor, a fortress of land dropped out of origin, like five parts too big drifted away to sea.*, 2020. Pearls, paillettes, plastic, metal beads, fabric, sequins, plastic, thread, and metal; 65 $^{11}/_{32}$ x 31 $^{1}/_{2}$ x 17 $^{23}/_{32}$ inches (166 x 80 x 45 cm). Courtesy of the artist. © Rina Banerjee. Photo by Dario Lasagni.

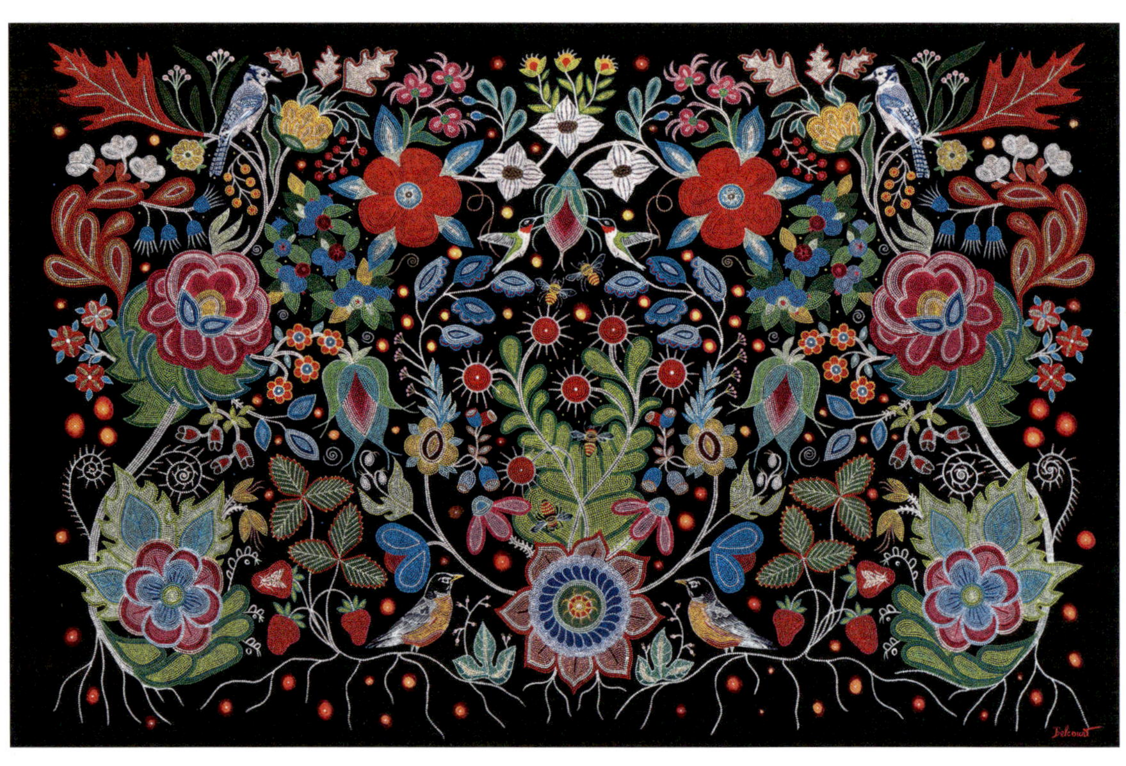

CHRISTI BELCOURT, *This Painting Is a Mirror*, 2012. Acrylic on canvas, 73 x 107 inches (185.4 x 271.8 cm). Indigenous Art Collection, Crown-Indigenous Relations and Northern Affairs Canada. © Christi Belcourt. Photo by Lawrence Cook.

Christi Belcourt

APIHTÂWIKOSISÂNISKWÊW FROM MÂNITOW SÂKAHIKANIHK
(LAC STE. ANNE, ALBERTA, CANADA), 1966

Life is big. The earth in constant motion. We are gifted only short moments that string together to make up an all-too-short life. And we pass through this ever-changing life, unable to freeze a single moment. But despite our short lives, our spirits come from the eternal. We are part of the energy that rises and moves and leaves before fire comes. We are part of the tides that rise like our chests taking in air. Over and over, generation to generation.

And I think about the coming generations. I wonder what kind of world they will be born into. I wonder not only about our species, but also about all species. I think about the baby bears or the baby birds coming to this world in the next five hundred years, I wonder if they will have clean air to breathe and lands to be born into? What about the fish in a thousand years, will they have clean water to be born into?

These questions and my love for the earth drive my life and my art. I want people to be reminded of the innocence within themselves, when they loved with their full hearts. And to be reminded of the beauty in themselves. To act with generosity and kindness toward the "stranger," to act as though every child was their own and every living being was deserving of dignity. I want people to fight for this world, by invoking their inner passions to guard and protect the goodness that still exists, and participate in actions that protect people, all species and all places. Before we need to call for justice. And I would hope that my art might inspire some of this reflection, to remind people of the mystery of this world, our interconnection with all living species, and to remind people that their own spirit was born from love, as all this world was born.

> — Excerpt from "Artist Statement," originally published in *Christi Belcourt* (Thunder Bay, ON: Thunder Bay Art Gallery/Carleton University Art Gallery, 2020), 17. Reprinted courtesy of the author, Thunder Bay Art Gallery, and Carleton University Art Gallery.

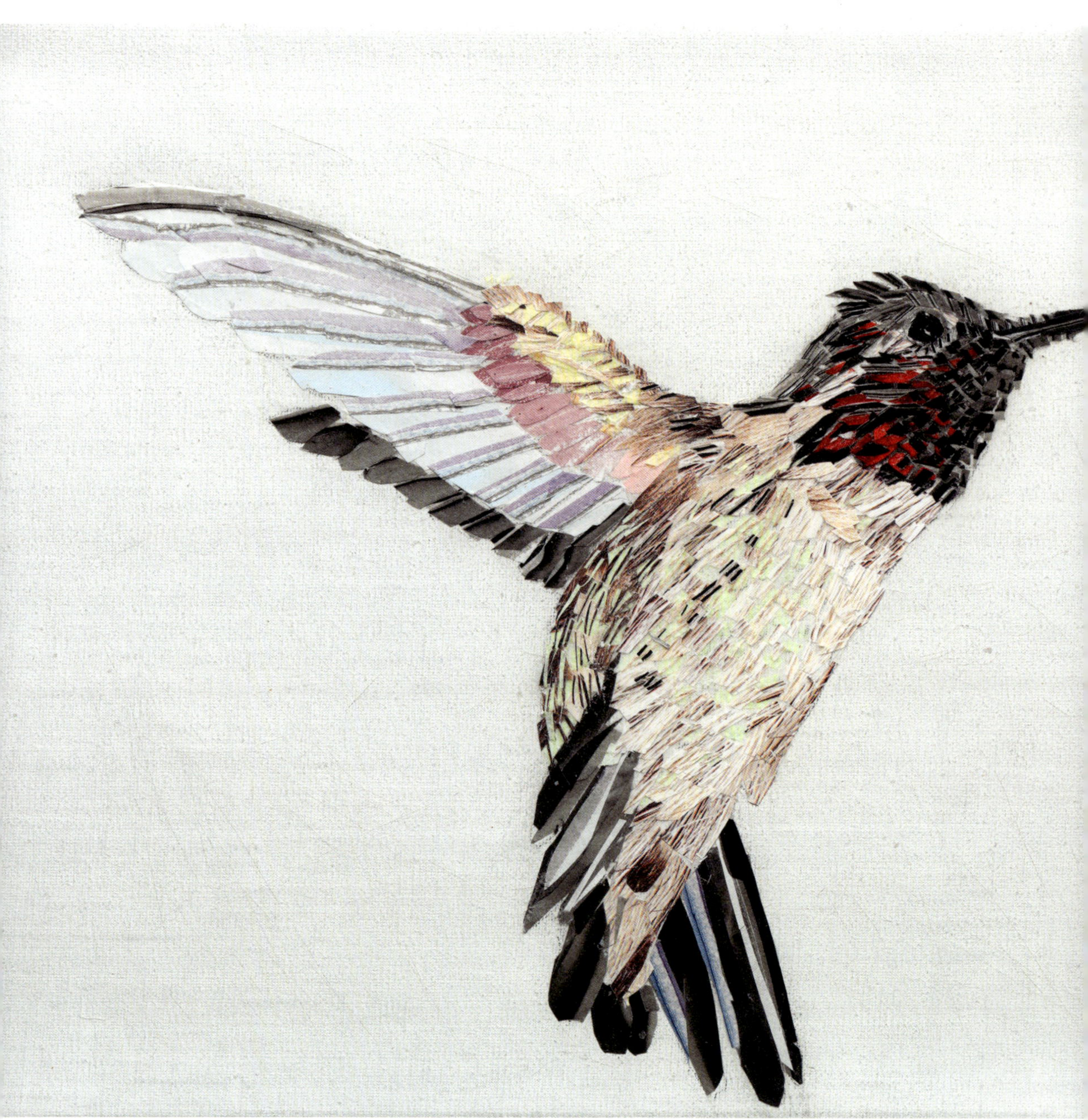

María Berrío

BORN IN BOGOTÁ, COLOMBIA, 1982

I'm fascinated by the complicated relationship between humankind and nature, and this theme always seems to enter into my works. Human beings, as fragile and impermanent as we are, can fathom gods, the infinite, and the supernatural. We even think of ourselves as supernatural, in the sense that our consciousness somehow sets us apart from the rest of nature—that there is Nature, and then there is Humanity, as if we were not simply nature becoming aware of itself. Perhaps this is an inevitable side effect of consciousness. Either way, it has led to odd, complex notions that I enjoy exploring in my art.

Nature is often seen as either a remorseless force to be fought against or an idyllic Eden. Neither of these concepts give nature, in all its vastness, much depth. We all readily admit to its complexity and yet don't allow our relationship to be much more than an oversimplified one: a romanticized, unrealistic portrait of a people utterly at one with their surroundings, or heroes at war with an implacable foe. I try to imagine worlds where these distinctions are swept away, utopias where nature and humankind are on equal terms.

MARÍA BERRÍO, *Joyas Voladoras* (detail), 2021. Collage with Japanese paper on linen, 9 x 12 inches (22.9 x 30.5 cm). Courtesy of the artist and Victoria Miro. © María Berrío. Photo by Bruce White.

The more we've distanced ourselves from nature, the more we've shown our interconnectedness with it—skyscrapers, planes, and factories have only proven that while we are fragile, so too are the ecosystems we inhabit and have encroached upon. It is an interesting paradox that industrialization has revealed our complete oneness with nature: the climate crisis makes it clear how inseparable we are from it. The lines we have artificially drawn between the human domain and the natural world are constantly in flux, and it's a blurred, shifting borderland, where one often overtakes the other. Wilderness becomes cities and farmlands, while wildlife around Chernobyl thrives and Angkor Wat becomes a jungle.

Ultimately, during an age when technology and screens often serve as blinders, it is imperative that we regain our more intimate knowledge of nature. Birds and certain plants and trees often make appearances in my works for a variety of reasons, but I like to think they serve as a reminder of the wider world. I like to think that art also plays a part, that, as a Dadaist saying goes, art allows us to realize that nature is greater than art.

We tend to lock ourselves into our own worlds, beholden to our own joys and sorrows, ignoring our part in the larger circle of life as if we could remove ourselves from it. By distancing ourselves mentally, technologically, and materially from nature, we not only fail to see nature's wonder but also our own place in that wonder. We are but one fragment of something far grander than our laughter and sadness—part of a wondrous continuum.

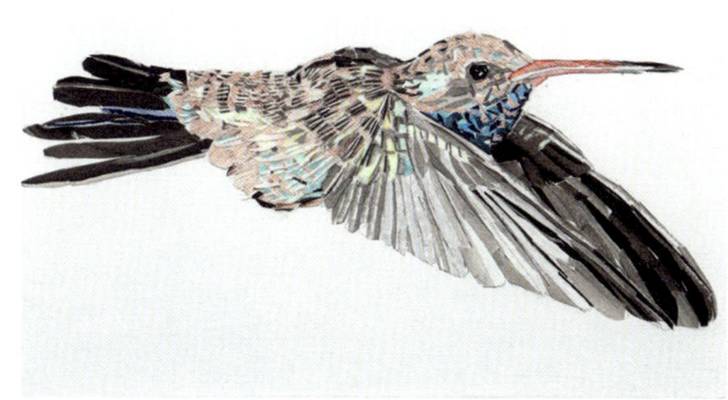

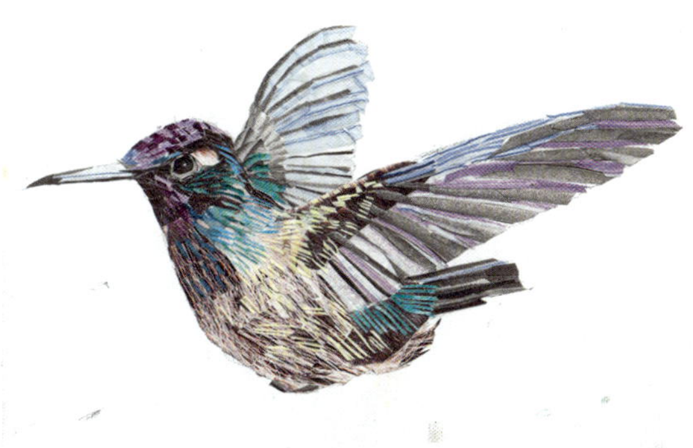

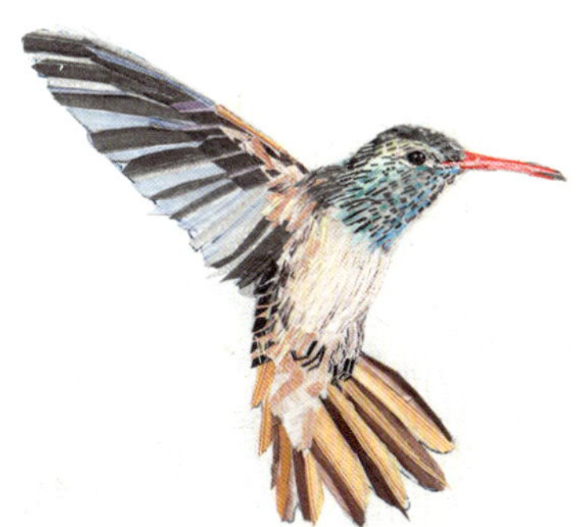

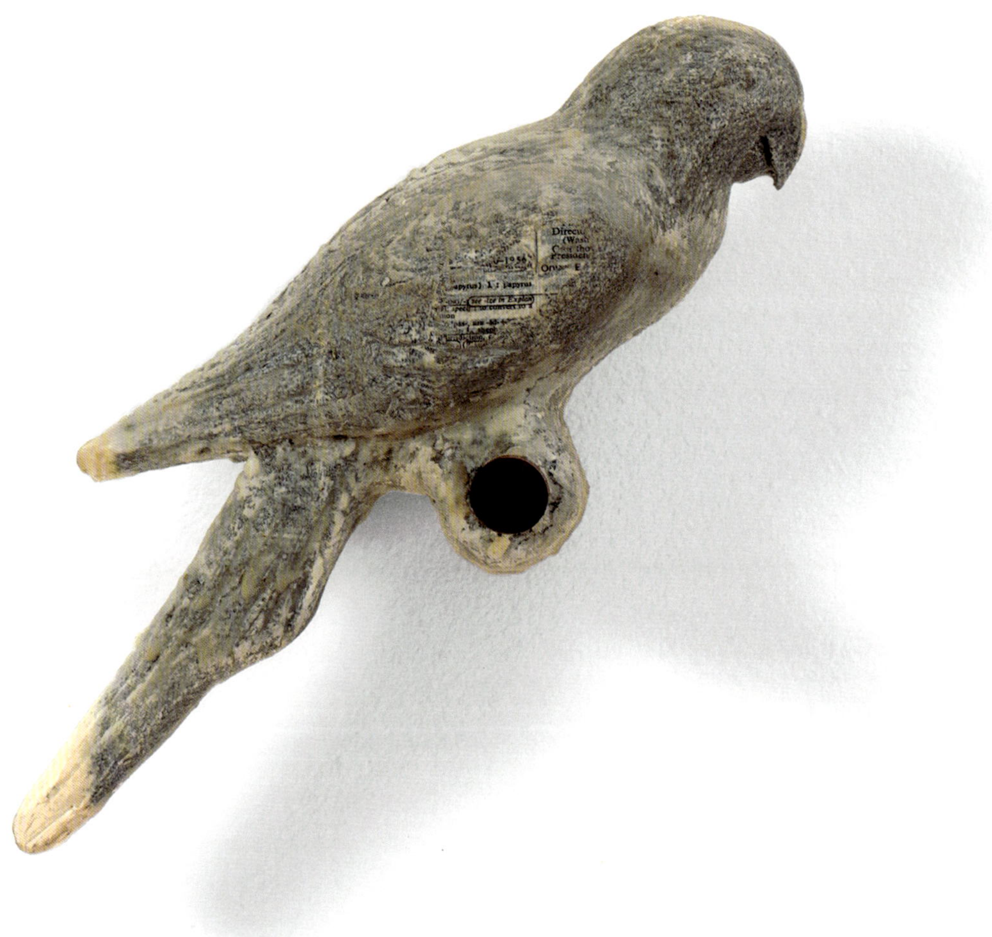

MEL CHIN, *The Bird is the Word* **(North Carolina Variation)**, 2001/2019. *Webster's Third New International Dictionary*, beeswax, and cherrywood; 11 x 10 x 6 inches (27.9 x 25.4 x 15.2 cm). Lent by The David and Alfred Smart Museum of Art, The University of Chicago; Purchase, The Paul and Miriam Kirkley Fund for Acquisitions. © Mel Chin.

Mel Chin

BORN IN HOUSTON, TEXAS, 1951

Some Words on a Bird
Before the WORD arrived
The spirit of the land had a voice
Of color of cackle of hoots and whistles
And it filled the forests.

The choruses of song and snarl
Spoke to those who walked the land
Who expressed their histories without
written word.
No contracts for negotiation
All abided by wordless law.

Then Others arrived and brought the WORD
Framed in devotion to follow:
Full exploitation of all dominions.

This new spirit over the land
Carved away the bounty of life
True believers exempted from negotiation
Between birds and bison, plants, and trees,
A strange exchange for eternal life.

In a brief span of time,
Color, cackle, hoots, whistles extinguished.
The forests were hewn and seasons muted.

Hard to describe
What was gone by the time I arrived
The spirit of the land not guided by words
Undone by a spirit that lived by the WORD.

The Bird is the Word
Webster compiled many words to
lament extinction.
None were chosen from the weighty
tome,
The Third International edition had
A brief entry,
A tiny illustration
Of a parakeet.
Steeped in boiling wax,
Chilled, leaving entries entombed
Texts turned to stone on thin pages.

Like the culture that carved away
the bounty of life,
Word after word was pared away
Leaving a lexicon of loss perched in
solitude.

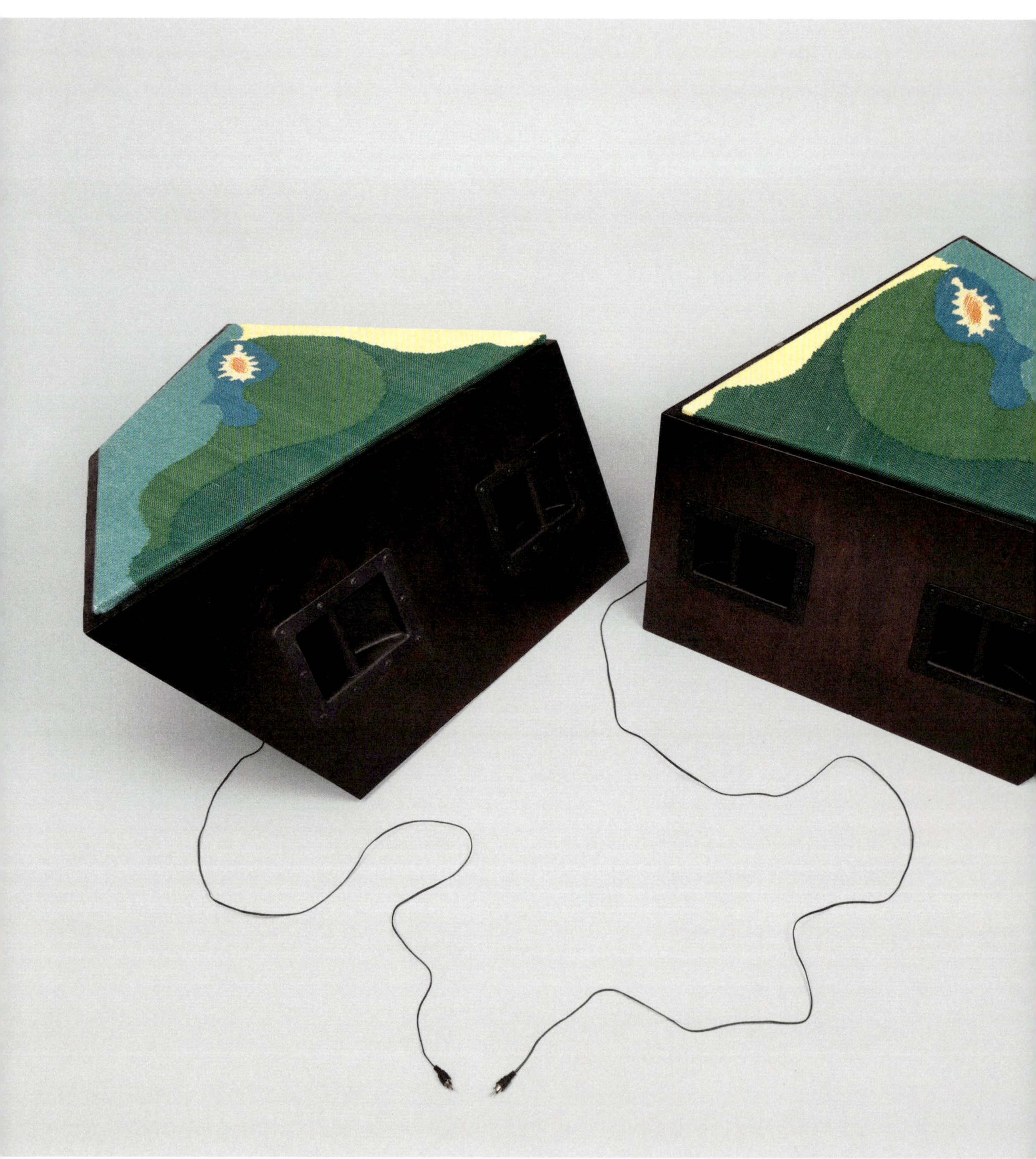

Never Forever

"A Diamond Is Forever," how to measure what
is forever gone?
Two big diamonds with handwoven fabric
covering speaker cabinets.
Assemble one,
Break another.
On one, play back a full concert of creatures'
recreated voices
A crystalline presentation, a tapestry of sounds.
The other a field of isolated voices,
The debris of that music.

The Cabinets of Conuropsis carolinensis

Audubon's graphical illustrations,
The palette for woven color, a special
cocklebur diet,
Yields patterns stretched as grills over acoustic
speakers
Set in shard-shaped cabinets.
Consider them coffins, chunks of the large
diamond
Lie on the floor resonating
Through the warp and wefted colors,
A species' imagined esprit de corps.
Softly audible
Reconstituted dispirited squawks
As bytes transmit through wires
Technological approximation of mating calls
With none living to deliver,
And none living to respond.

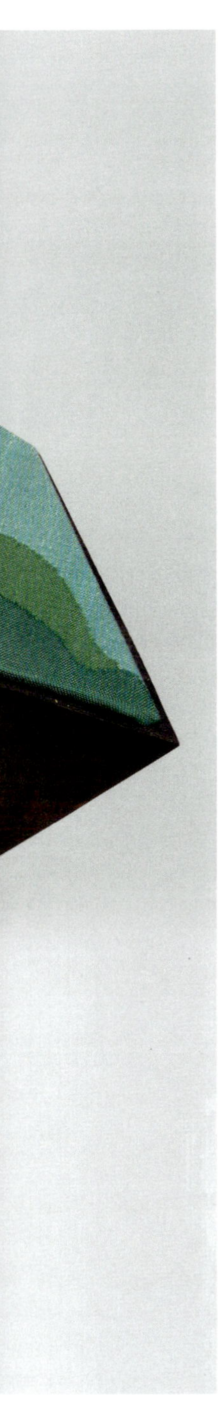

MEL CHIN, *Never Forever: The Cabinets of Conuropsis*, 2022. Wood, lacquer, pigment, steel, hand-woven tapestry (dyed cotton), and electronic/audio components; 60 x 24 x 42 inches (152.4 x 61 x 106.7 cm) (overall). Courtesy of the artist. © Mel Chin.

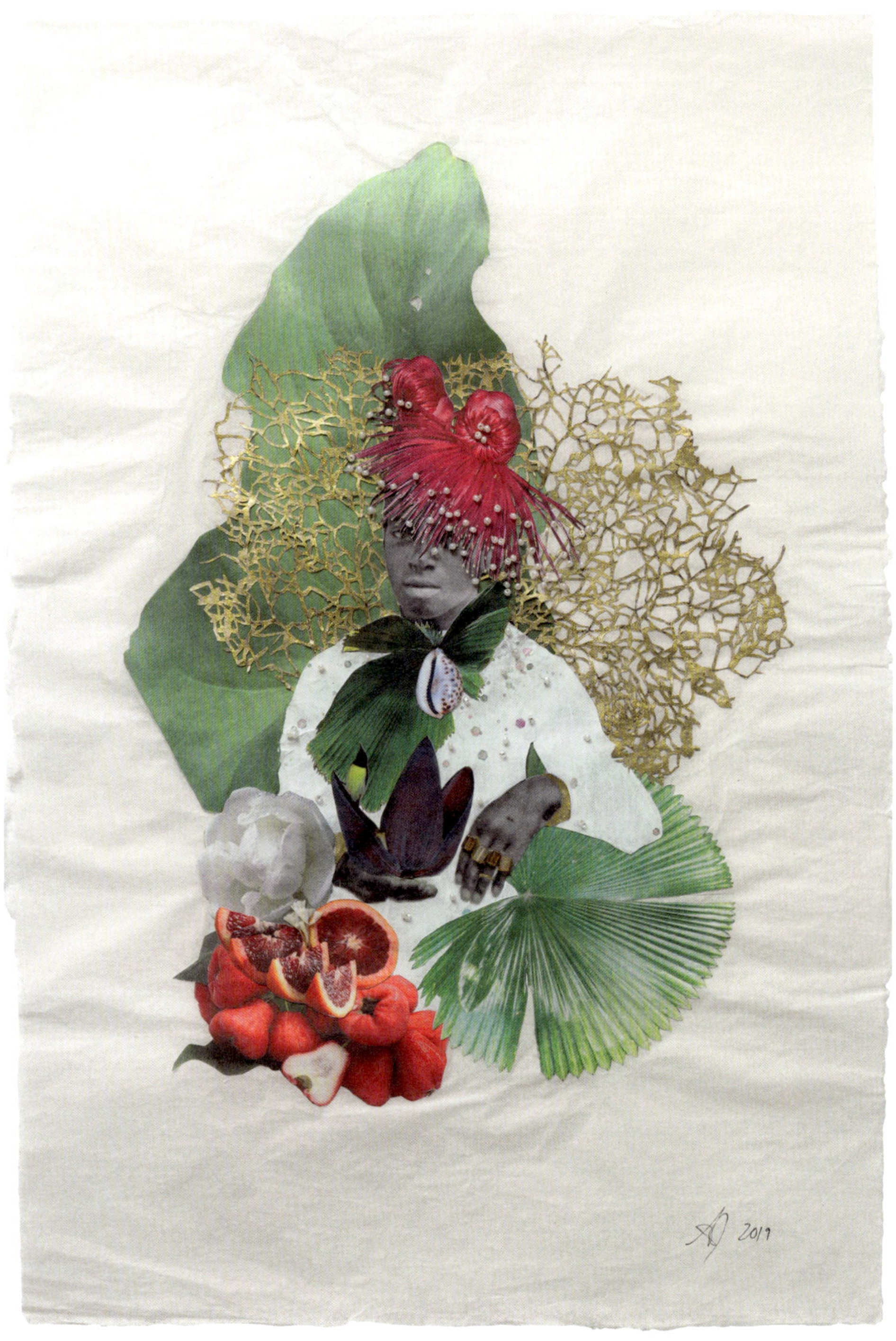

Andrea Chung

BORN IN NEWARK, NEW JERSEY, 1978

Archival photographs have always been an integral part of my practice; I have long been interested in considering who owns images of people who did not own themselves or who could not have conceived of the consequences of the consent they gave, if any was given at all. I am mindful of complications around the photographer's gaze but also my own, and that of the viewer, when I use these images in collages.

I am also deeply interested in herbal culture and the relationships between the people in these images and the land. During the transatlantic slave trade enslaved Black women carried their herbal and medicinal knowledge along with them to the "New World." Enslaved midwives were able to provide women with the power of resistance in the form of reproductive autonomy. With the use of herbs like pennyroyal, guinea-hen weed, and the peacock flower, Black midwives provided other enslaved women with assistance in contraception, pre- and postnatal care, and even abortifacients, allowing them to reclaim what they could of their personhood.

I combine these two lines of thought in collages. In the series *VEX* and *Colostrum*, I use foliage to protect private moments, to imagine these women reclaiming ownership of their own images, to disrupt the colonial gaze, and to interrogate the multiplicity of the relationships the enslaved had to the Earth: it both bound and freed them.

ANDREA CHUNG, *Untitled (Sisters of Two Waters)*, 2019. Collage, glitter, and beads on paper handmade from traditional birthing cloth; 12 x 9 inches (30.5 x 22.9 cm). Image courtesy of the artist and Tyler Park Presents. © Andrea Chung. Photo by Michael Underwood.

ANDREA CHUNG, *House of the Historians*, 2022. Sugarcane bark and leaves, sweetgrass, excelsior and floral twine; dimensions variable. Courtesy of the artist and Tyler Park Presents. © Andrea Chung. Installation view: "everything slackens in a wreck," June 1–August 20, 2022, Ford Foundation Gallery, New York. Photo by Sebastian Bach.

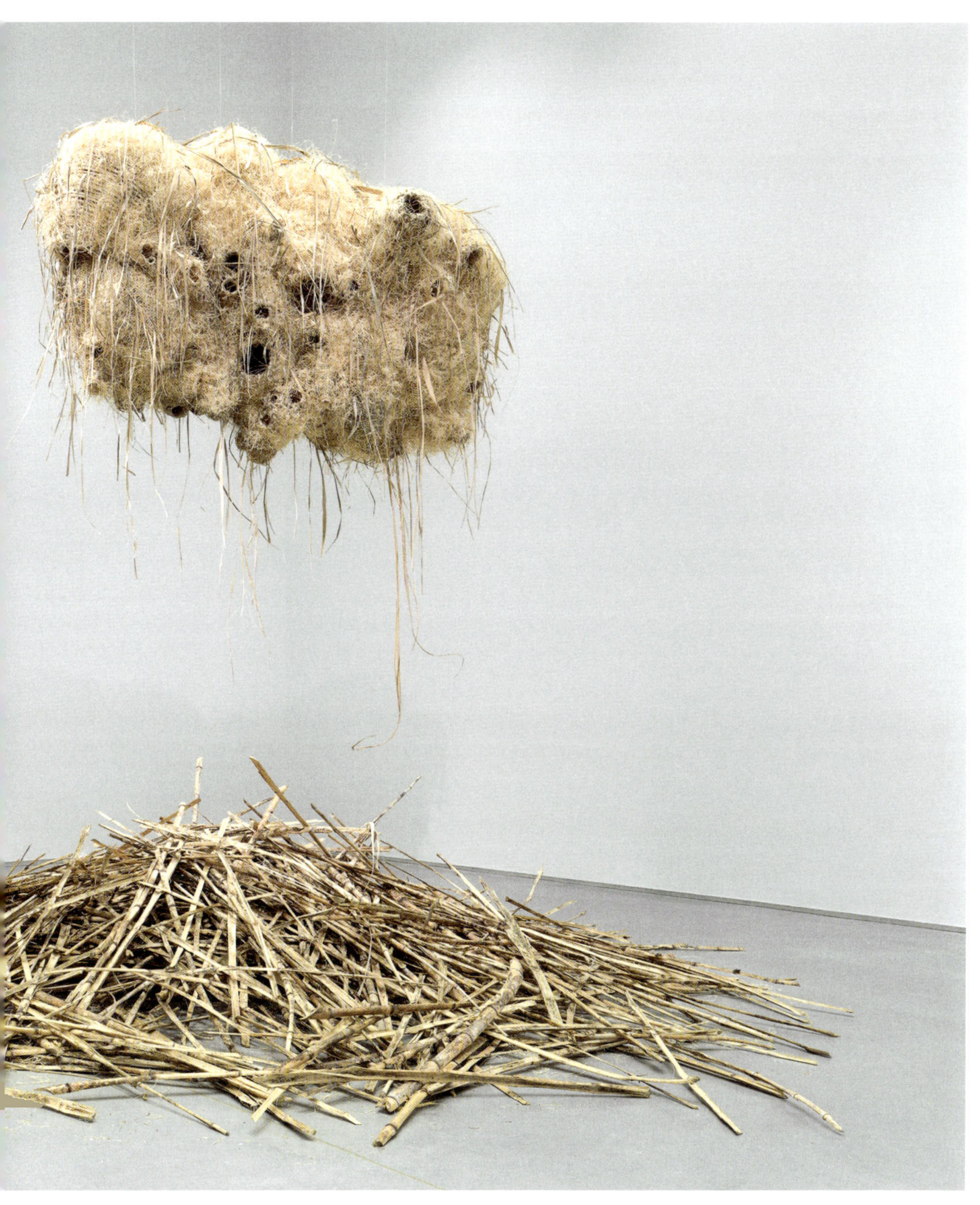

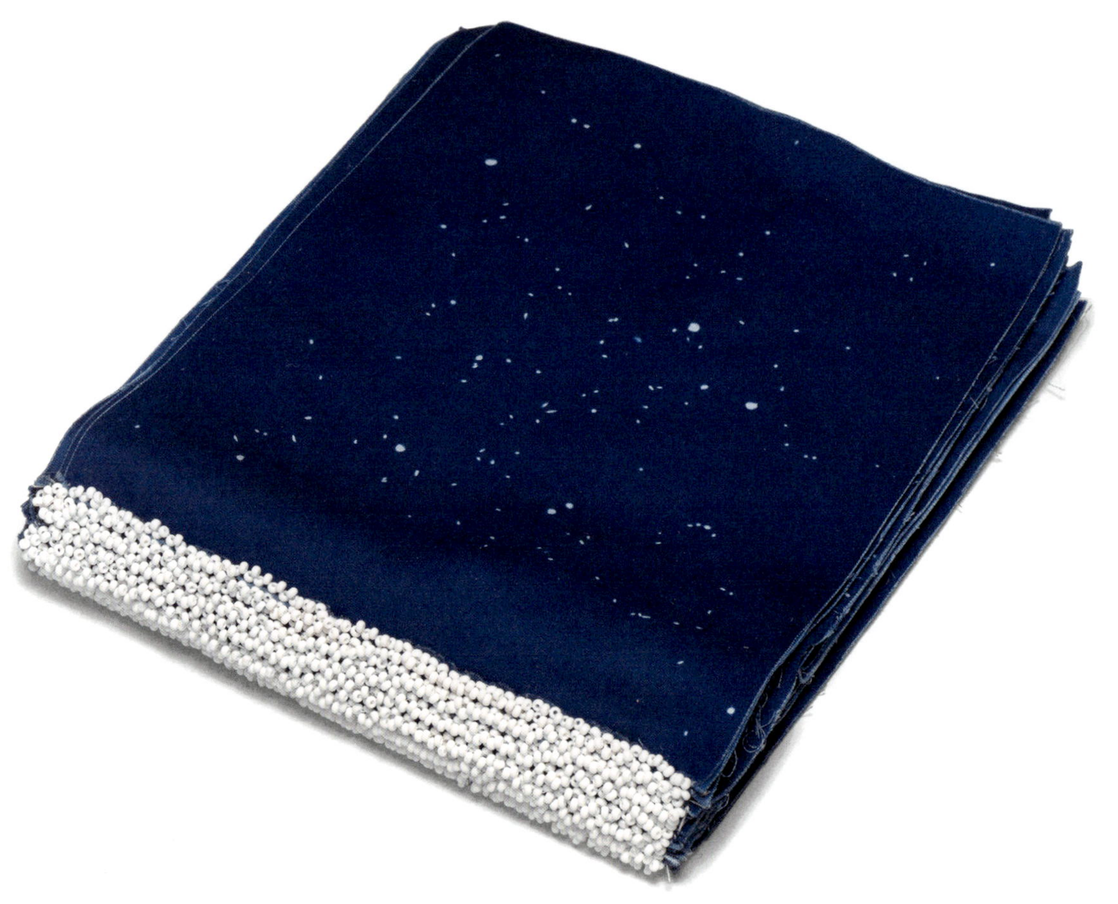

Sonya Clark

BORN IN WASHINGTON, DC, 1967

Freedom looks like the dark night sky and everyone having a chance to look at it, wonder about it, and know it.

— Chanda Prescod-Weinstein,
The Disordered Cosmos

We are star seeds. Eyes to the sky, I still hold child-wonder in my heart from the first time. Far from the city fog of light, in the vast dark velvet, on a camping trip, the stars felt close like warm freckle-kisses on my brown skin. Unfathomable distant suns tethered to my pupils.

A belonging.

I was taught the stars are our ancestors. Each distant sun, a soul, a relative written in our DNA. All that vastness contained in us. We are star seeds.

Freedom is feeling the stars within. Let's start the story there.

Claiming our connection to this universe is a freedom and a responsibility. This is what Harriet Tubman and so many other freedom fighters have, an innate resistance to the unfreedoms perpetrated by others, a reclamation of what rightly belongs to all. This work's title, *Heavenly Bound,* comes from the "Swing Low, Sweet Chariot" lyric, as a reminder: "But still my soul feels heavenly bound, coming for to carry me home." We are star seeds. We are "each other's magnitude and bond," as Gwendolyn Brooks wrote in her poetic homage to Paul Robeson.[1] Robeson himself understood what was at stake when he said the words that hang above my studio desk: "The artist must elect to fight for Freedom or for Slavery. I have made my choice. I had no alternative."[2]

Like tending the Earth, many hands have sprinkled vegetal seeds
on these cotton cloths infused with cyanotype, a combination
of two salts discovered by nineteenth-century astronomer John
Herschel in a photography process made famous by botanist
Anna Atkins.

Many wrote this cloth book: artists, students, children, adults, those
who take freedom for granted, and those who do not, are all here.
Each hand is a palimpsest in blood and bone of ancestors. The
sunlight from our nearest star developed the photographs, shifting
the cloth from grass green to sand tan. Then, dipped in water, the
cloths turned magical blue. Speckles of white remind us where
the seeds were. Constellations emerge, random arrangements, all
of which exist somewhere in the cosmos. Among them is a Big

Dipper, the Drinking Gourd, Harriet's guide to freedom. Because, she too, an astronomer, never forgot to claim her freedom. Because even though their lifetimes never crossed, she lived what Toni Morrison proclaimed: "The function of freedom is to free somebody else."[3]

These cloth pages are bound together with glass seed beads. Beads made from the substance where sea meets land. Beads, small as seeds, named as such, remind us of the sustenance the soil provides. And so the stories of our freedoms are bound together. Earth to Sun to water—a whole ecosystem. We are star seeds.

The "we" extends beyond the human.

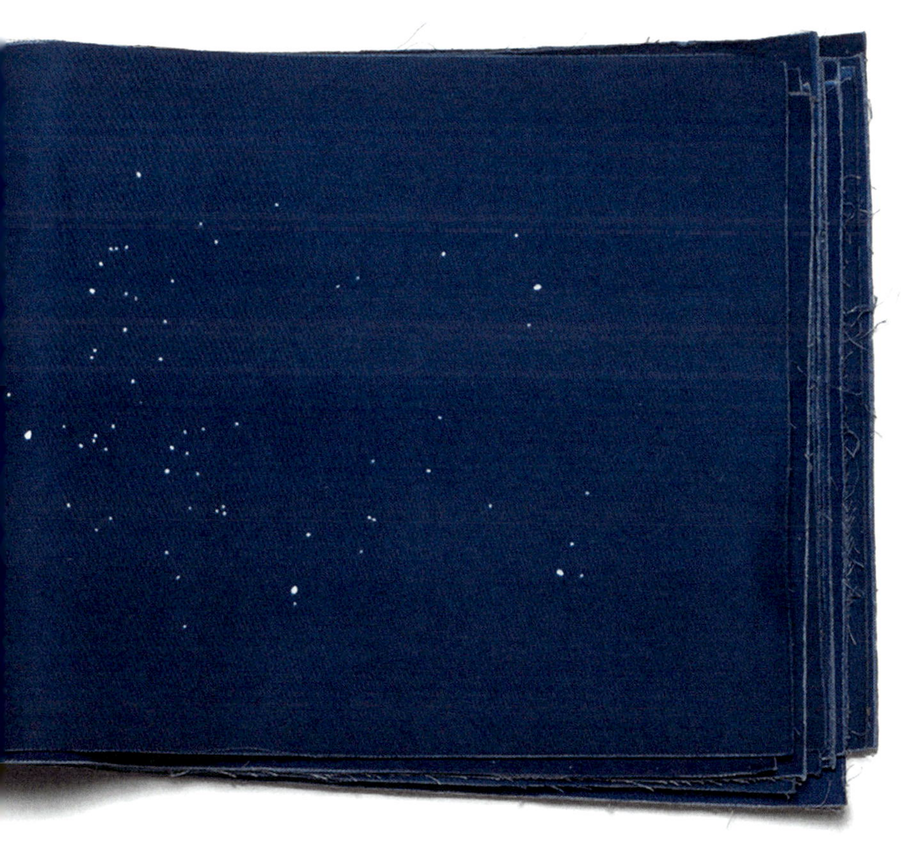

1 Gwendolyn Brooks, "Paul Robeson," in *The Essential Gwendolyn Brooks*, ed. Elizabeth Alexander (New York: Library of America, 2005), https://poets.org/poem/paul-robeson.

2 Paul Robeson, *Here I Stand* (1958; repr., Boston: Beacon Press, 1998), 52.

3 From Toni Morrison's 1979 Barnard College commencement address, "Cinderella's Stepsisters"; reprinted in *Medium*, Zora editors, August 7, 2019, https://zora.medium.com/toni-morrison-in-her-own-words-562b14e0effa.

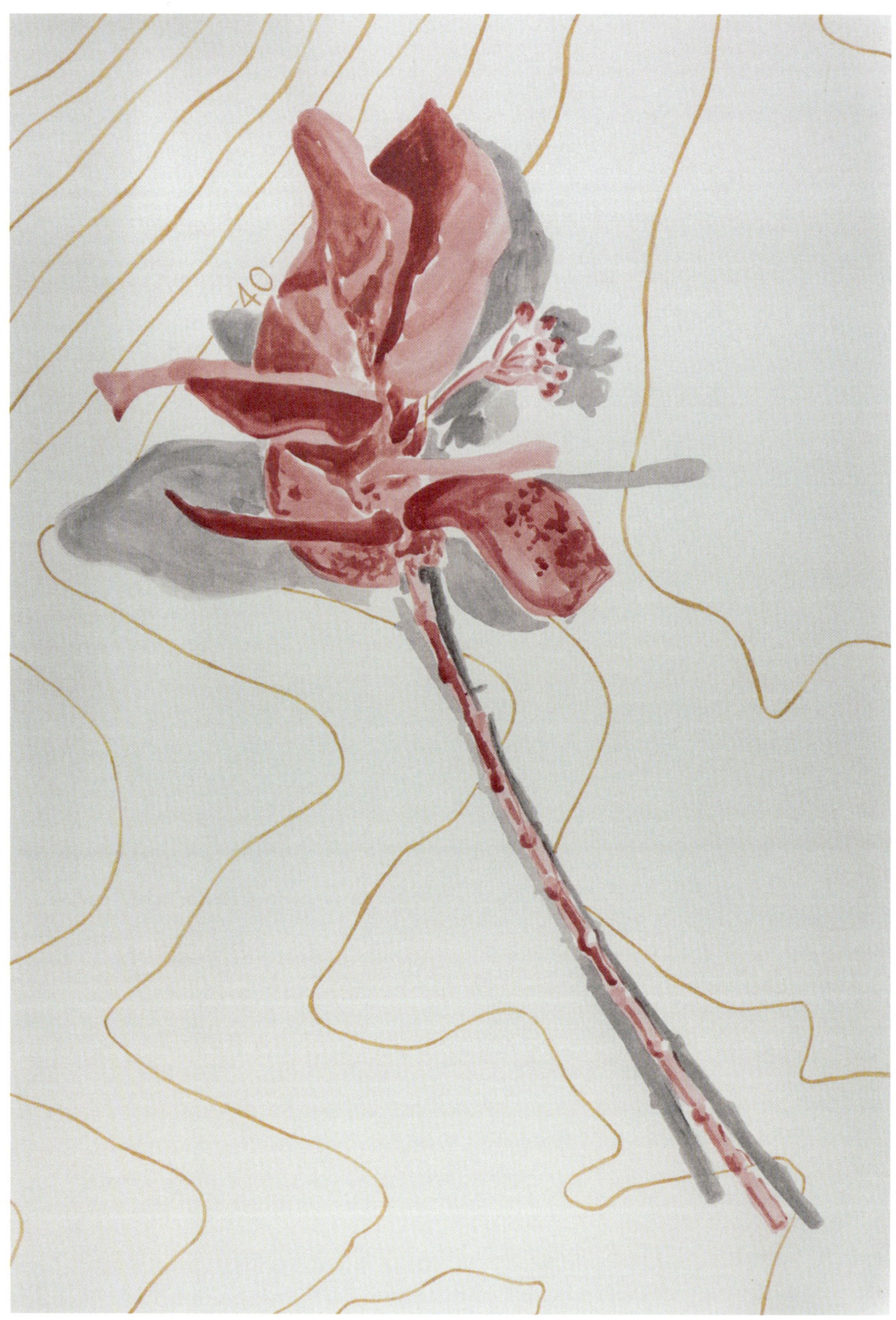

ANNALEE DAVIS, *From a Garden of Hope: French Cotton (Calotropis procera)*, 2021–2022. Ink and latex on paper, 25 x 18 inches (63.5 x 45.7 cm). Courtesy of the artist. © Annalee Davis. Photo by Russell Watson, RStudio.

Annalee Davis

BORN IN ST. MICHAEL, BARBADOS, 1963

I often spend time walking, as a ritual act through radically distorted landscapes that have been adapted over centuries to the needs of a global marketplace and maximizing profits without thought to the unfree, Indigenous, indentured, and enslaved labor or the ongoing degradation of the soil.

This body of drawings evolved out of my ongoing research exploring post-plantation economies and post-extractive ethics. For this work, the focus is more specifically on Walkers Reserve in the parish of St. Andrew in the Scotland District on the east coast of Barbados. The original plantation, called The Hope, was established by Richard Powrey. At his passing, in 1662, Judith Powrey, his widow, sold half of the two-hundred-acre plantation to her second husband, John Barwick, whom she was about to marry.[1] Three plantations were eventually adjoined—the Ford Plantation, The Hope, and Sandy Hill—into one massive 666-acre plantation in the early 1700s, which became Walkers, renamed after its owner George Walker.

This estate shifted from one extractive economy to another, from a seventeenth-century sugar plantation to a silica sand quarry in the late twentieth century. Situated within the extensive dune community named Long Pond, for the past five years it has been undergoing yet another transition into a permaculture site with some areas reserved for conservation. It has been renamed Walkers Reserve.

From a Garden of Hope is a collection of drawings atop hand-drawn contour lines reproduced from a geological survey revealing the natural features of the Scotland District. The drawn contour

1 Woodville Marshall, *Of Halls, Hills and Holes: Place Names of Barbados* (Bridgetown, Barbados: Barbados Museum and Historical Society, 2017), 372.

lines continue onto each meditative rendering of wild botanicals, becoming an inaccurate mash-up—a kind of counter mapmaking exercise that logs overlooked yet commonplace plants found growing across this transforming landscape. *From a Garden of Hope* recalls one of the early names of this collated land and is connected to a living apothecary planted at Walkers Reserve, which is focused on the reproductive and post-reproductive health of women, as well as being a live first aid kit. It honors the many women who would have lived and worked on this land.

Blue vervain, horseweed, clammy cherry, feather finger grass, and French cotton are among the many botanicals I found growing on Walkers Reserve's sandy soils. They form part of a small herbarium of plants I have collected, pressed, photographed, and made drawings of as a gesture of care through careful observation. In part, this work advocates for a practice of "innerseeing"—as opposed to the historic role of the overseer common on all plantations—offering other routes to connect with the ground beneath our feet while fostering a more intimate relationship with such heavily mediated lands.

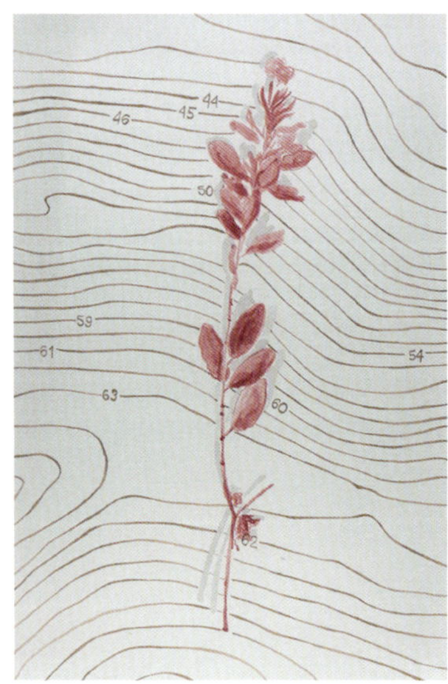

From a Garden of Hope: West India Tea (Capraria biflora)

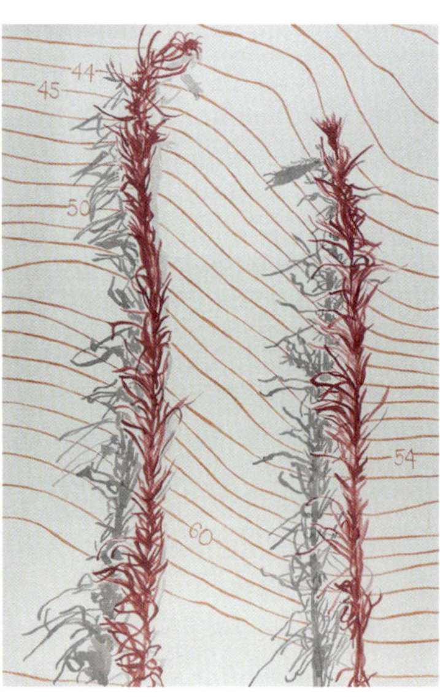

From a Garden of Hope: Horseweed (Conyza canadensis)

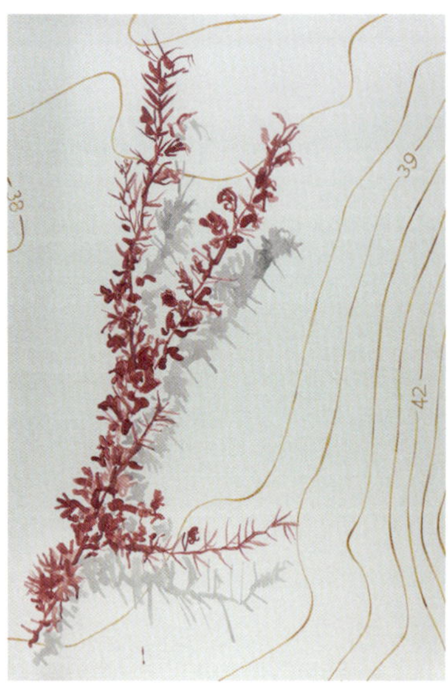

From a Garden of Hope: Acacia tortuosa

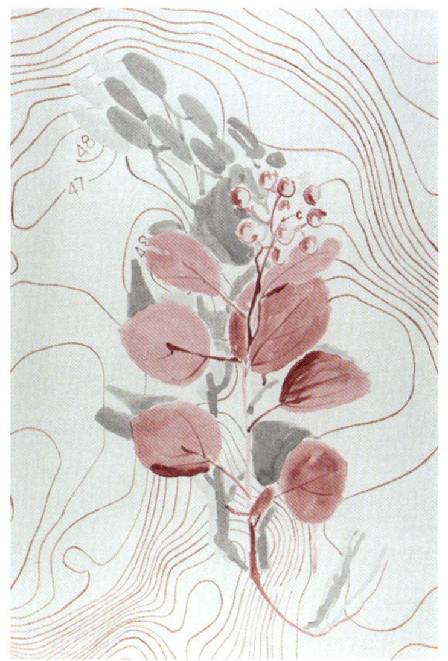

From a Garden of Hope: Clammy Cherry (Cordia dentata)

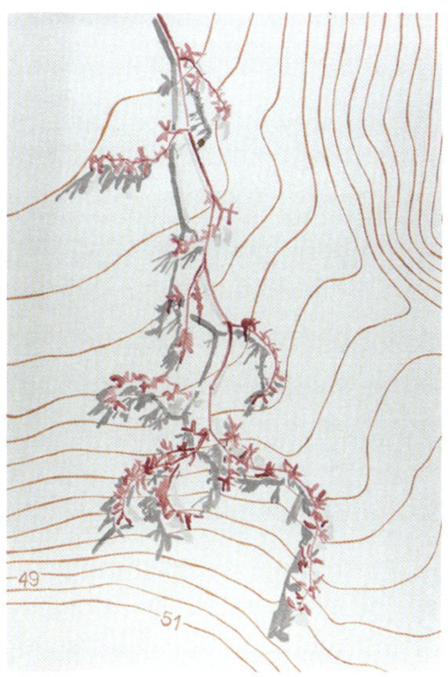

From a Garden of Hope: Chickenweed, Purslana Family (Portulaca quadrifida)

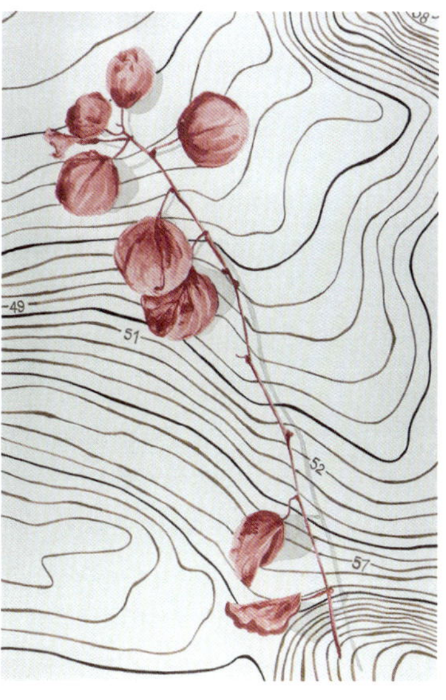

From a Garden of Hope: Wompuh, Seaside Yam (Ipomoea pes-caprae)

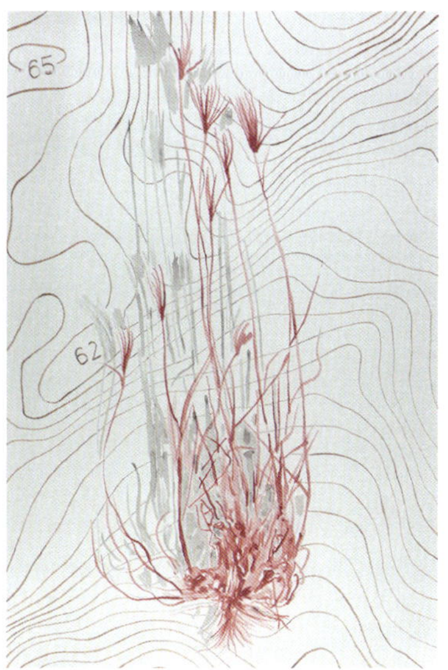

From a Garden of Hope: Feather Fingergrass (Chloris barbata)

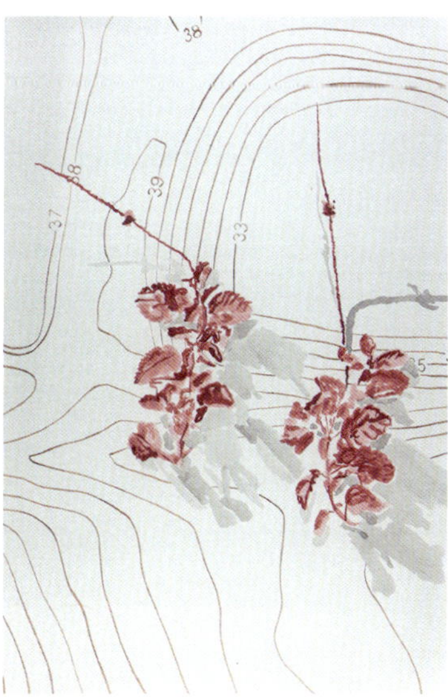

From a Garden of Hope: Blue Vervain (Verbena hastata)

ANNALEE DAVIS, Selections from ***From a Garden of Hope***, 2021–2022. Ink and latex on paper, 25 x 18 inches (63.5 x 45.7 cm) (each). Courtesy of the artist. © Annalee Davis. Photo by Russell Watson, RStudio.

Tamika Galanis

BORN IN NASSAU, BAHAMAS, 1979

I was a peculiar child, consumed with anthropomorphizing plants and animals and the idea of talking to ghosts. I spent most of my childhood squirreled away with my head in books or playing in the dirt, building imaginary worlds. I came of age in Nassau, Bahamas, in a culture whose folklore is rooted in African folklore—full of trickster spirits represented by plant and animal life, straddling our reality and life beyond the veil—and this is the foundation upon which my practice is built. I was left to my own devices for entertainment: climbing trees, eating fruit plucked directly from the plant, running wild with my hair untamed, getting buried in the sand, having to be dragged out of the sea, and playing with all manner of tiny life-forms. As an adult, my departure from this carefree immersion in nature nearly killed me, turning often to it now continues to enrich my life. My artistic process has benefitted largely from—I'd even venture to say, is dependent upon—my tenacious pursuit of rewilding.

I have the incredible fortune, at midlife, to be back in my childhood home, where my grandmother has lovingly attended to our own "Garden of Eden" for more than thirty years. Regular communication with Spirit and spirits (in the Caribbean vernacular, "sperrit") is no longer an idea, but a confirmed, constant, and enriching truth. Once attuned to it, my ancestors, and the ancestral collective, often make their presence known; it's a common daily occurrence for several species of heron to cross my path, along with frogs roaring songs announcing rain, cranes sauntering atop our hedge, scores of crows standing guard on the wall, beautiful Bahamian boas, and lately—marking a new migratory pattern—flocks of black ibises strutting their stuff. Everyone shows up as an answer to a question. I see spirits in the plants and flowers, and feel their absence when I am torn from my daily communion with whatever is blooming brightly: bougainvillea, frangipani, yellow elder, allamanda, oleander, and the "medicine" of the big trees like the poui and the silk cotton.

Catching Shadow came into being in answer to an otherworldly call to make work in honor of the silk cotton tree—observed throughout the Americas as a repository for the dead and a meeting place of realms. Not indigenous to the Bahama Islands, its existence here is speculatively attributed to travel between Africa and The Bahamas during the transatlantic slave trade. Silk cotton trees are characteristically identifiable by their aboveground root system, and, in some cases, thorns, which ascend the trunk of trees that aren't fully mature. Historical travel guide accounts date them as approximately two centuries old by the early 1900s.

Catching Shadow is the story of an Obeah woman who petitions a silk cotton tree for a spirit bound there, inadvertently freeing more than she intended. The spirits in the film, aptly represented by photographs, which are essentially light and shadow, point to another historical reference to "shadow" as self-representation, as in Sojourner Truth's famous inscription underneath her photograph on her cartes de visite: "I sell the shadow to support the substance." The film is based on an actual folk practice outlined in Martha Warren Beckwith's book *Black Roadways*, which documents inquiry into Jamaican folkways from 1919 to 1924. I collaborated with Dr. Charlotte Henay and Princess Pratt to birth this iteration of the film, earthside—both practitioners and conjurers in their own right, they bring a special medicine of their own to this project. Charlotte Henay, whose voice features in the film, introduced me to the idea of leaving offerings at the foot of the silk cotton tree several years ago. The prose in the film is from her manuscript, currently titled, *All of My Peoples' Bones Are Here: Talking to the Dead as Poiesis for Afro-Indigenous Futurities*. While many schools of thought point to the silk cotton tree as a portal to the past, Charlotte teaches that it is a doorway into and through spaces, places, and time as nonlinear. Princess Pratt, who plays the role of the Obeah woman in the film, is a storyteller, musician, and an avid steward of our folkways and keeper of our culture—in innumerable ways—whose drumming while filming was so potent that it invoked a trancelike state on several occasions. Princess recently penned a story about the silk cotton tree as a portal, "Anansi and the Silk Cotton Tree."

Catching Shadow was filmed on sacred ground in Adelaide Village, New Providence, Bahamas, which was established in 1832 by the first Africans in the Bahama Islands who had been liberated from enslavement on ships en route to the Americas from Africa post abolition. When we arrived at Adelaide to scout trees for filming, we approached a tree with roots smaller than average for its size, touching it and asking it to identify itself. It answered in true anthropomorphic fashion by delivering a finger prick from the one lone thorn remaining on a tree that was long past maturity.

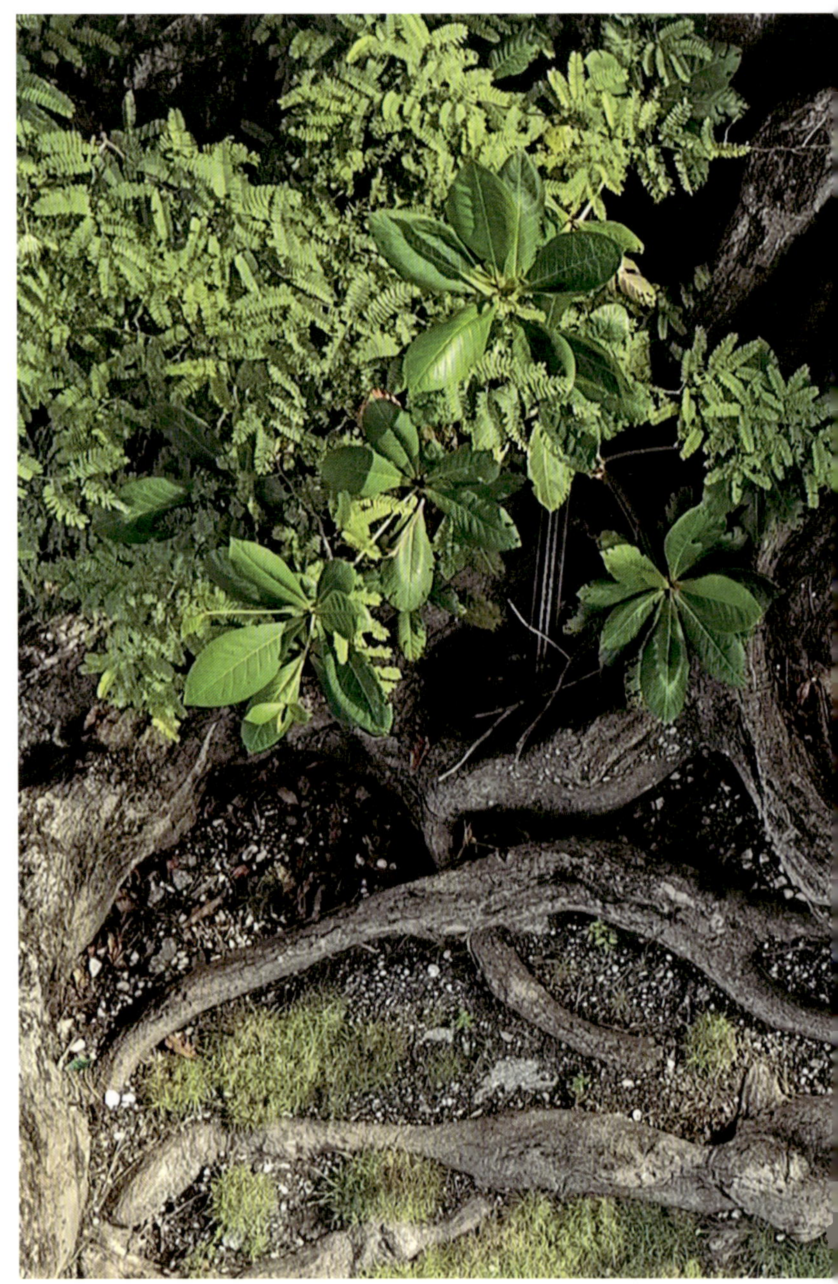

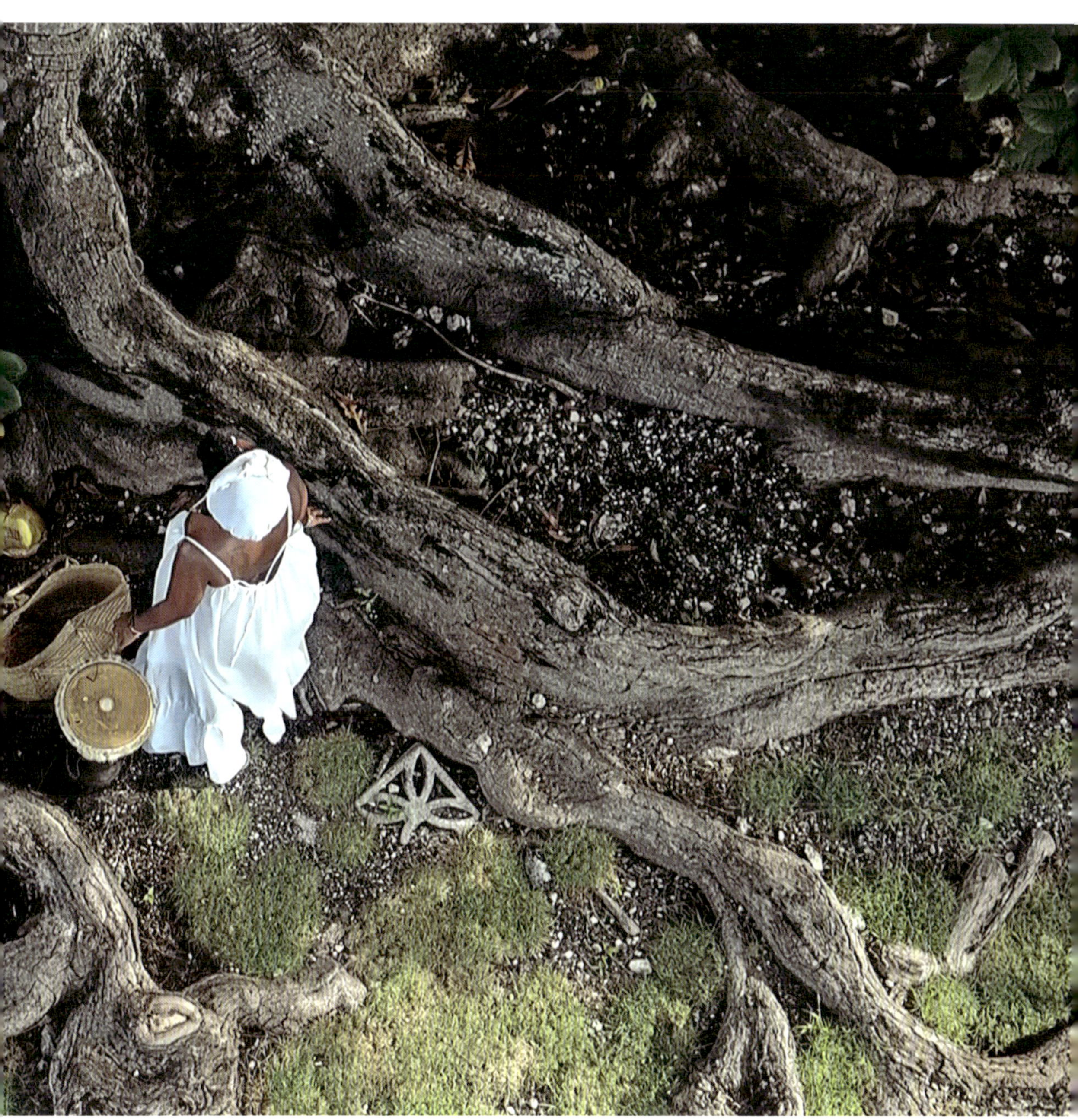

TAMIKA GALANIS, Still from *Catching Shadow*, 2021. Video (color, sound), 6:02 minutes. Courtesy of the artist. © Tamika Galanis.

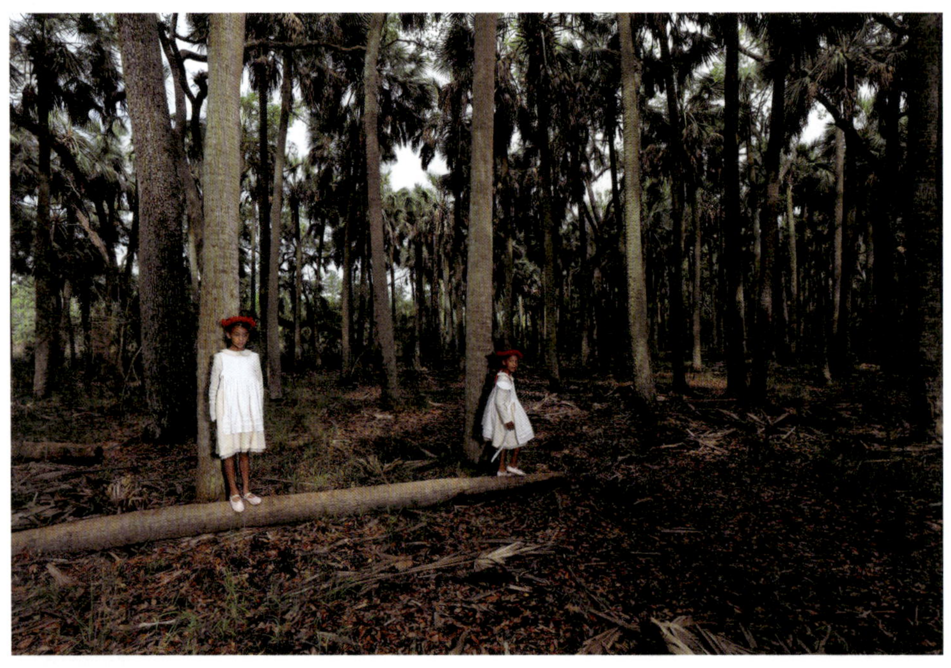

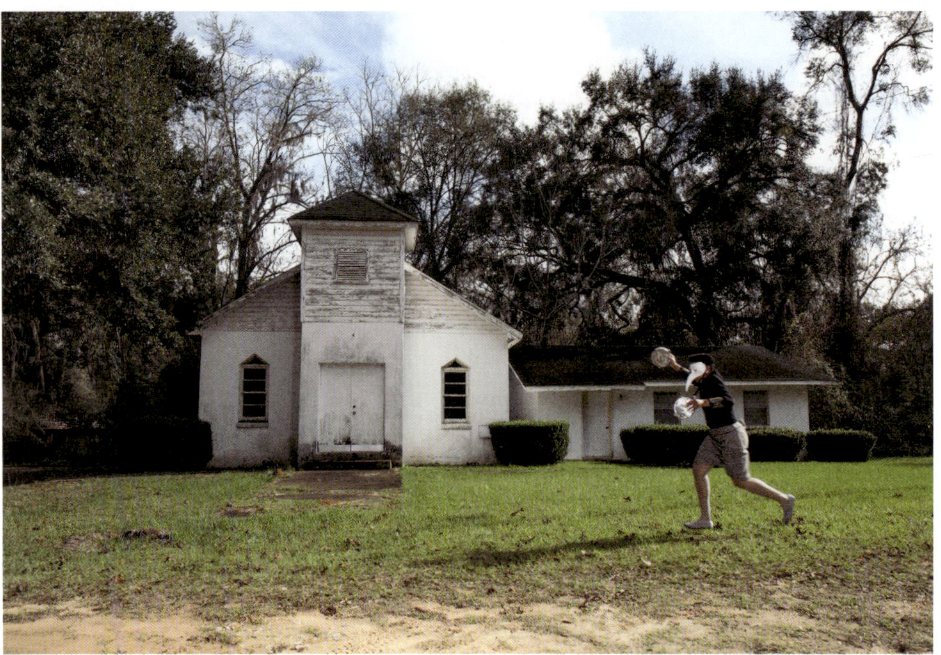

Allison Janae Hamilton

BORN IN LEXINGTON, KENTUCKY, 1984

My relationship to nature is fundamental to who I am. My experience of community, family, self, and culture are all inextricably linked to the natural environment. I was born in Kentucky, raised in Florida, and my maternal family's farm and homestead is nestled in the rural flatlands of West Tennessee. I come from a long line of Tennessee women who were hunters, farmers, and fisherwomen, quilters and midwives. As a child, I spent most planting and harvest periods on the farm in Tennessee, as we came up from Florida to help with whatever crop was being planted or coming in. Most of my childhood memories of Tennessee involve some sort of outdoor chore, like collecting guinea fowl eggs, feeding the hunting hounds, helping to burn trash or to pick corn and beans. As an adult, I remain drawn to the haunting stillness of the flat farms cutting into the West Tennessee woodland landscapes.

Being raised primarily in Florida, a dramatic, yet incredibly vulnerable landscape, taught me how landscape can be at once powerful and delicate, and it continues to influence the way I think about place. Today I split my time between New York City and the Red Hills of northern Florida's swamp country, just on the other side of the Georgia border where sprawling live oak trees with dripping Spanish moss, swamp pines and magnolias, alligators, cottonmouths, and prehistoric great blue herons are staples of the landscape. When I work in Florida, the local materials become part of my sculpture practice, and my friends and family are often characters in my photographs and films. Our time spent together in our region's cypress swamps, oyster flats, and red clay trails informs the context and concepts of the art that comes out of it.

ALLISON JANAE HAMILTON, *Sisters, Wakulla County FL*, 2019. Archival pigment print, edition 2/5, 24 x 36 inches (61 x 91.4 cm). Collection of the Nasher Museum of Art at Duke University, Durham, North Carolina. Museum purchase with funds provided by The Durham (NC) Chapter of The Links, Incorporated; 2021.13.2. © Allison Janae Hamilton. Courtesy of the artist and Marianne Boesky Gallery, New York and Aspen.

ALLISON JANAE HAMILTON, *When the wind has teeth*. from the series *Sweet milk in the badlands.*, 2015. Archival pigment print, edition 1/5, 40 x 60 inches (101.6 x 152.4 cm). Collection of the Nasher Museum of Art at Duke University, Durham, North Carolina. Museum purchase with funds provided by The Durham (NC) Chapter of The Links, Incorporated; 2021.13.3. © Allison Janae Hamilton. Courtesy of the artist and Marianne Boesky Gallery, New York and Aspen.

My artwork and methods of working are likewise inextricably linked to the land. Through the specificity of the landscapes I call home, I engage wide-reaching issues of life and land: of power, of politics, of a changing climate, and of the link between natural disasters and human-made disasters that give terrible environmental events their social and political meaning. What do hurricanes tell us about how landscapes and the populations living in them are valued? What might a reflection on North Florida's turpentine camps reveal about the economies borne out of the exploitation of lives and land? From the topics I explore to the materials I use—skins and feathers, mythic constellations, tambourines, moss, image projections of majestic creatures and vermin alike—my work animates the land as a central protagonist of each narrative rather than a neutral backdrop. The centrality of landscape has always been the lens through which I approach the environment, both in life and in work.

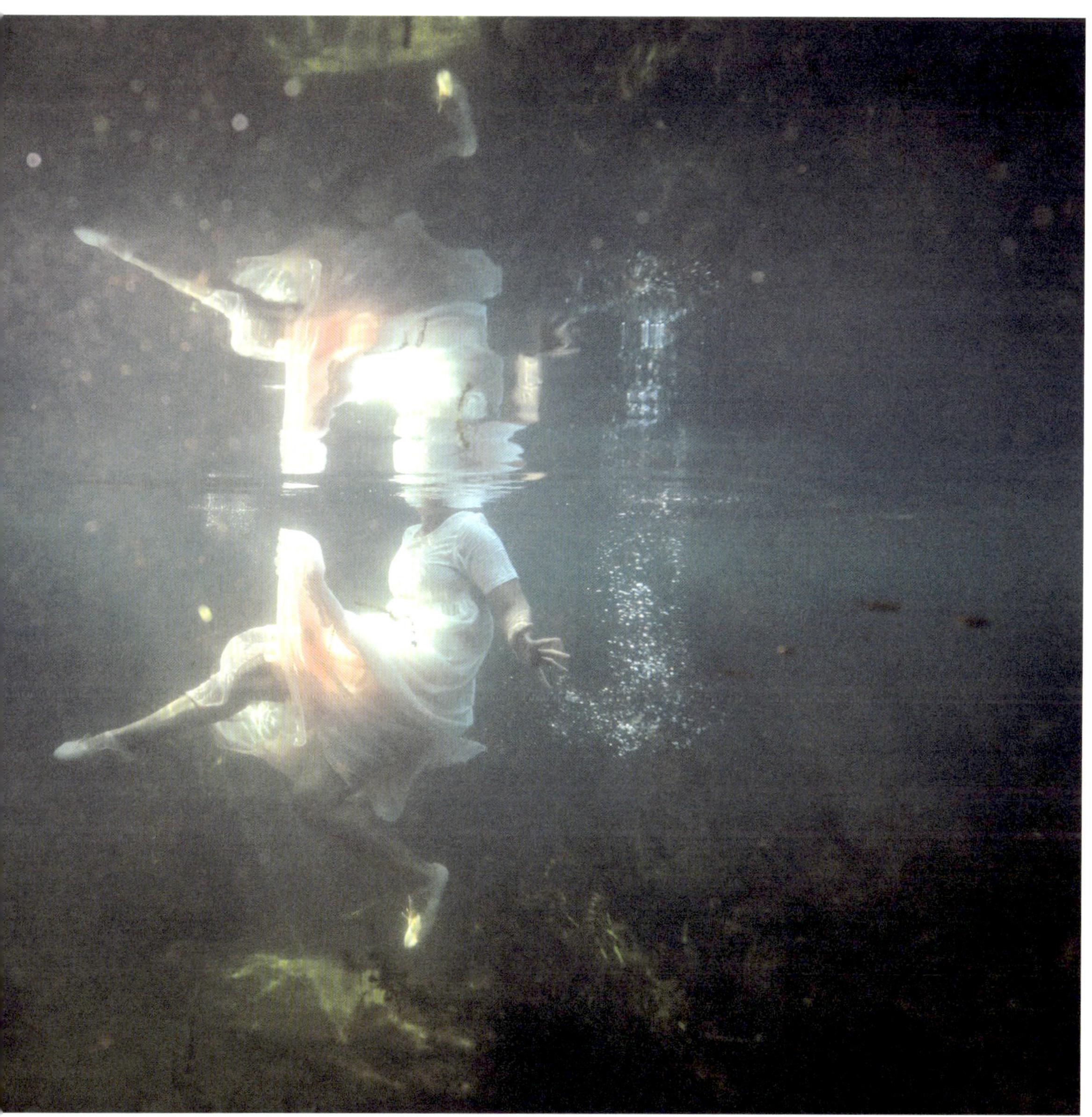

ALLISON JANAE HAMILTON, *Floridawater II*, 2019. Archival pigment print, edition 5/5, 24 x 36 inches (61 x 91.4 cm). Collection of the Nasher Museum of Art at Duke University, Durham, North Carolina. Museum purchase with funds provided by The Durham (NC) Chapter of The Links, Incorporated; 2021.13.1. © Allison Janae Hamilton. Courtesy of the artist and Marianne Boesky Gallery, New York and Aspen.

1 Barkley L. Hendricks, "Palette Scrapings," in *Barkley L. Hendricks: Birth of the Cool*, ed. Trevor Schoonmaker (Durham, NC: Nasher Museum of Art at Duke University, 2008), 89.

2 Hendricks, 113.

3 Susan Hendricks, phone conversation with Trevor Schoonmaker, May 26, 2022.

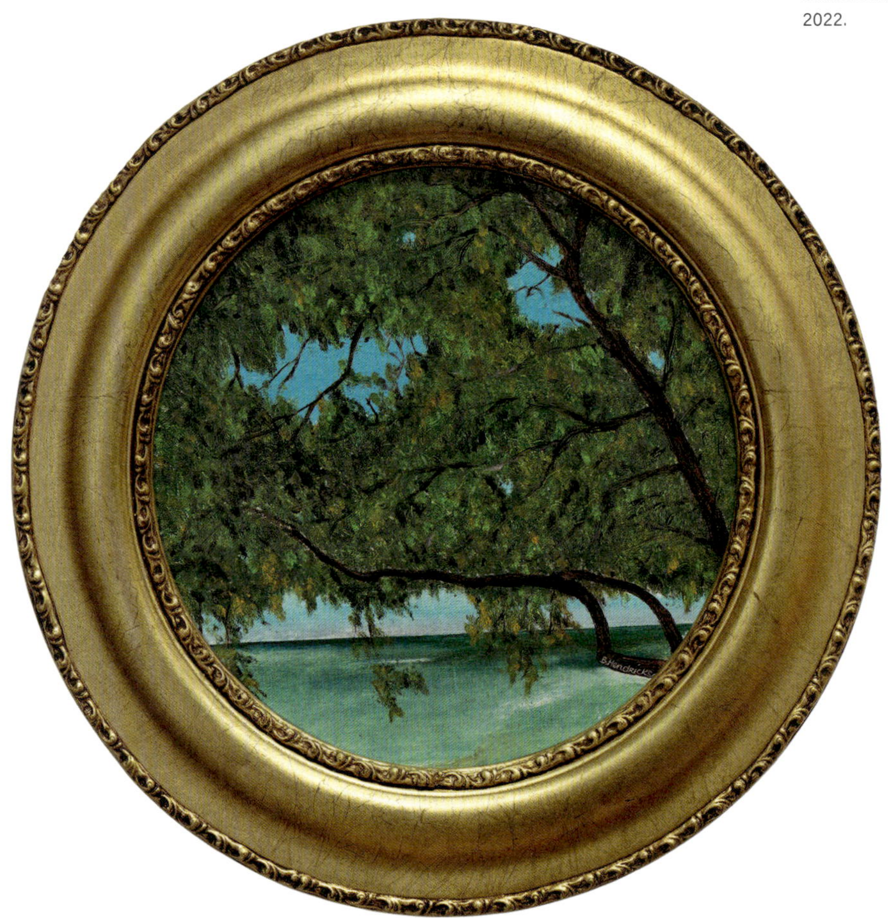

BARKLEY L. HENDRICKS, *Under Zim's Tree*, 1998. Oil on canvas, 17 $\frac{1}{4}$ inches (43.8 cm) (diameter). Collection of the Nasher Museum of Art at Duke University, Durham, North Carolina. Gift of Susan and Barkley L. Hendricks to commemorate naming Trevor Schoonmaker as Mary D.B.T. and James H. Semans Director of the Nasher Museum of Art at Duke University, 2020.6.2. © The Estate of Barkley L. Hendricks. Courtesy of The Estate of Barkley L. Hendricks and Jack Shainman Gallery, New York. Photo by Peter Paul Geoffrion.

Barkley L. Hendricks

BORN IN PHILADELPHIA, PENNSYLVANIA, 1945; DIED 2017

"…It is always a cool thing to find a place in the heat of the Jamaican countryside to sit and paint for several hours. It's a meditative event with oil and watercolor pigments. There are rapid dictations from Mother Nature where you have to pay attention. Actually some days are quite hot. How cool is that?! That is if tropical downpours do not chase me away from my chosen task and topics or bombarding bugs don't crash-land in my wet paint or ants and other insects are not dining on me or my palette's cadmium and titanium colors."[1]

"When I sit down to paint, occasionally I am reminded of the history of Jamaica and its associations beyond my narrow perspectives of aesthetics. The roads and fields I find myself on and in have many stories to tell beyond my creative motivations and responses to what I see around me. Do I really have to say the history was an important footnote to some of the vistas and perspectives I have painted?"[2]

— Barkley L. Hendricks

"Painting landscape was the thing that brought Barkley the most satisfaction—that and playing the trumpet, even more than painting the figures. The figures were early on, but when he discovered those Jamaican landscapes, that was it. He was reborn."[3]

— Susan Hendricks

The group of works illustrated here is being shown together for the first time. *Happy Birthday (for Martin)* was painted in New London, CT, in 1982, and leafed at a later date. *Cocoa Pod from My Man Sammy* and *Judy's Uneaten Fruit* were both painted in Ghana in 1996, and leafed later that year in New London. *Sweet Sop Sue* and *Naseberries* were painted in Jamaica in 2009 and 2010 respectively, leafed in New London, and given by Barkley to Susan as Christmas gifts. Never before published, they have been hanging in private view in the Hendricks home.

— Trevor Schoonmaker, Nasher Museum Director

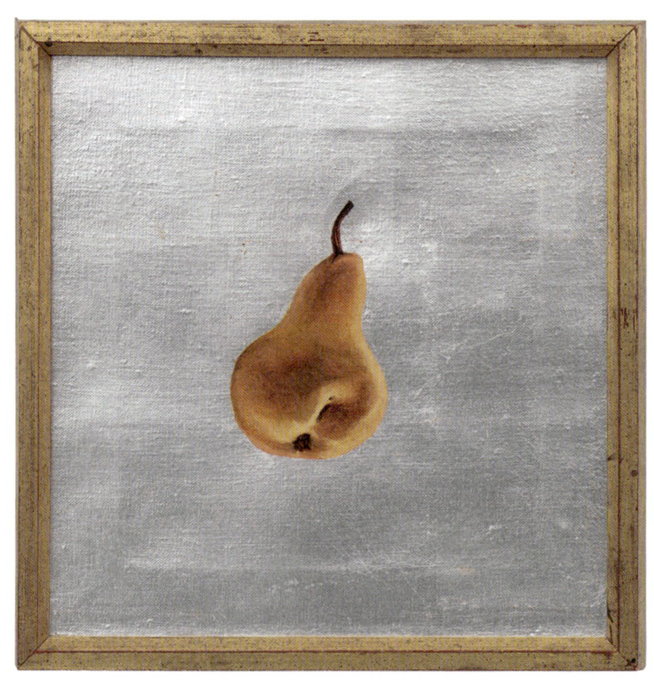

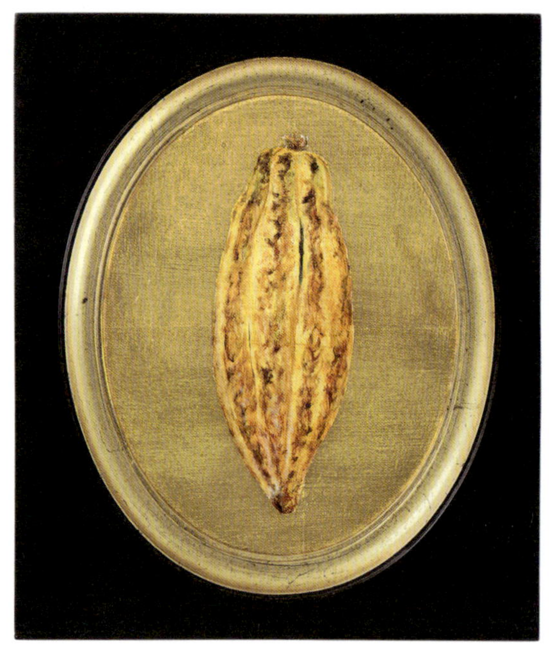

BARKLEY L. HENDRICKS,
Happy Birthday (For Martin),
1982. Oil and aluminum leaf
on linen canvas, 13 $\frac{1}{2}$ x 13 $\frac{1}{2}$
inches (34.3 x 34.3 cm).
Courtesy of The Estate of
Barkley L. Hendricks and
Jack Shainman Gallery,
New York. © The Estate of
Barkley L. Hendricks.
Photo by Dan Bradica.

BARKLEY L. HENDRICKS,
*Cocoa Pod from My Man
Sammy*, 1996. Oil and gold leaf
on linen canvas, 12 $\frac{7}{8}$ x 10 $\frac{7}{8}$
inches (32.7 x 27.6 cm).
Courtesy of The Estate of
Barkley L. Hendricks and
Jack Shainman Gallery,
New York. © The Estate of
Barkley L. Hendricks.
Photo by Dan Bradica.

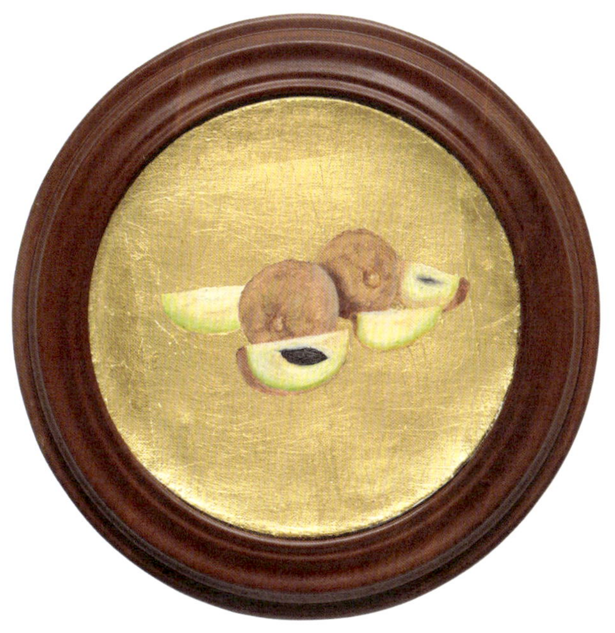

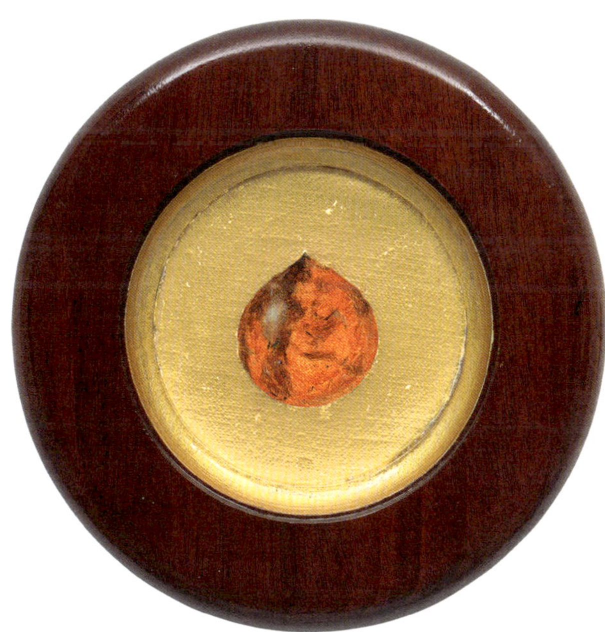

BARKLEY L. HENDRICKS, *Naseberries*, 2010. Oil and gold leaf on linen canvas, 11 $\frac{1}{8}$ inches (28.3 cm) (diameter). Courtesy of The Estate of Barkley L. Hendricks and Jack Shainman Gallery, New York. © The Estate of Barkley L. Hendricks. Photo by Dan Bradica.

BARKLEY L. HENDRICKS, *Judy's Uneaten Fruit*, 1996. Oil and gold leaf on linen canvas, 7 $\frac{1}{2}$ inches (19.1 cm) (diameter). Courtesy of The Estate of Barkley L. Hendricks and Jack Shainman Gallery, New York. © The Estate of Barkley L. Hendricks. Photo by Dan Bradica.

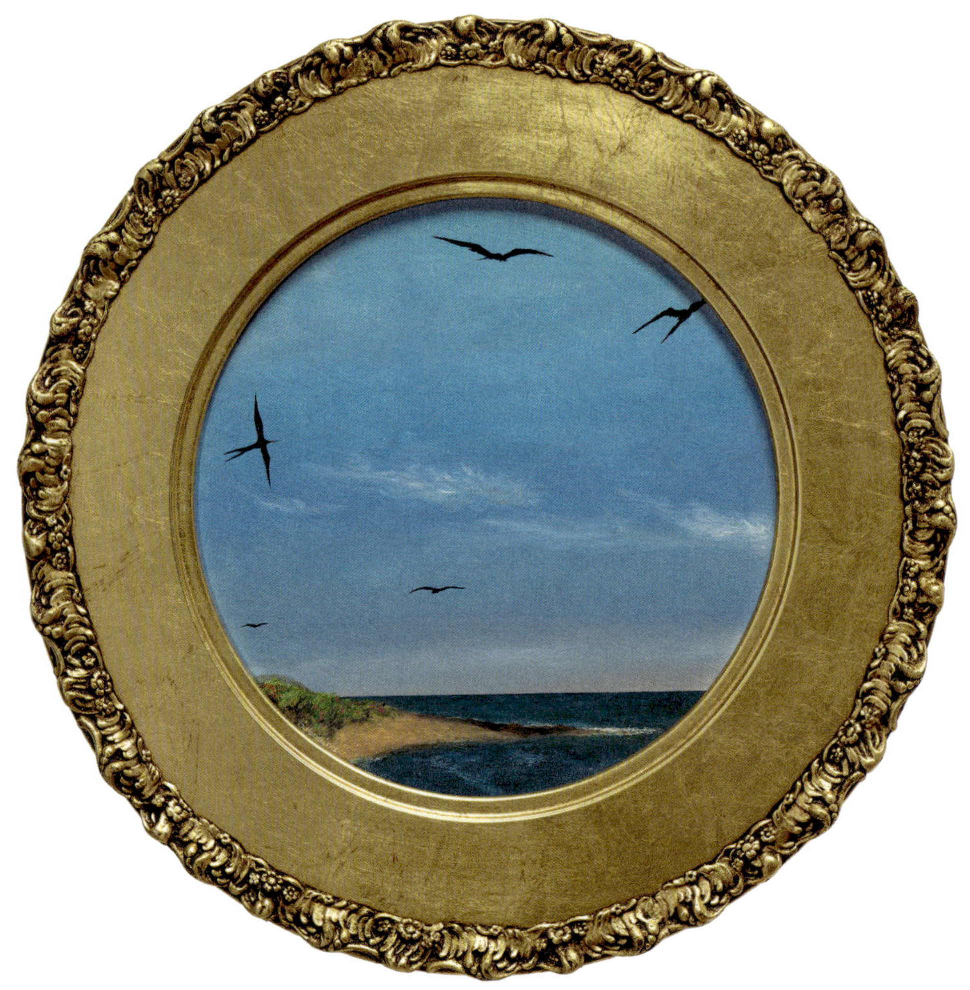

BARKLEY L. HENDRICKS, *Treasure Birds (Thoughts of Christmas)*, 1999. Oil on canvas, 21 ¹/₂ inches (54.6 cm) (diameter). Collection of the Nasher Museum of Art at Duke University, Durham, North Carolina. Gift of Susan and Barkley L. Hendricks to commemorate naming Trevor Schoonmaker as Mary D.B.T. and James H. Semans Director of the Nasher Museum of Art at Duke University, 2020.6.1. © The Estate of Barkley L. Hendricks. Courtesy of The Estate of Barkley L. Hendricks and Jack Shainman Gallery, New York. Photo by Peter Paul Geoffrion.

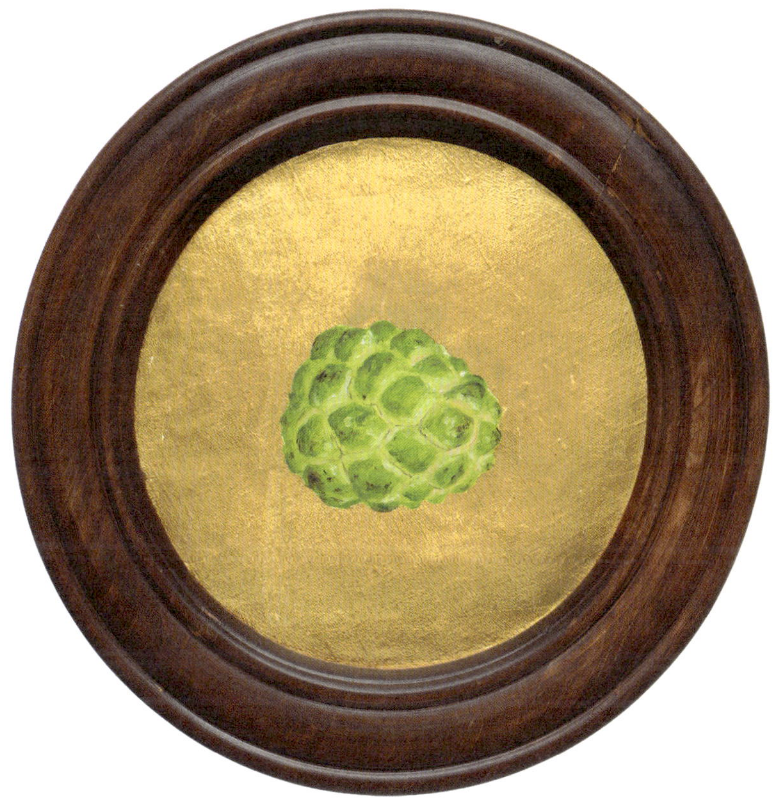

BARKLEY L. HENDRICKS, *Sweet Sop Sue*, 2009. Oil and gold leaf on linen canvas, $11\,^{1}/_{4}$ inches (28.6 cm) (diameter). Courtesy of The Estate of Barkley L. Hendricks and Jack Shainman Gallery, New York. © The Estate of Barkley L. Hendricks. Photo by Dan Bradica.

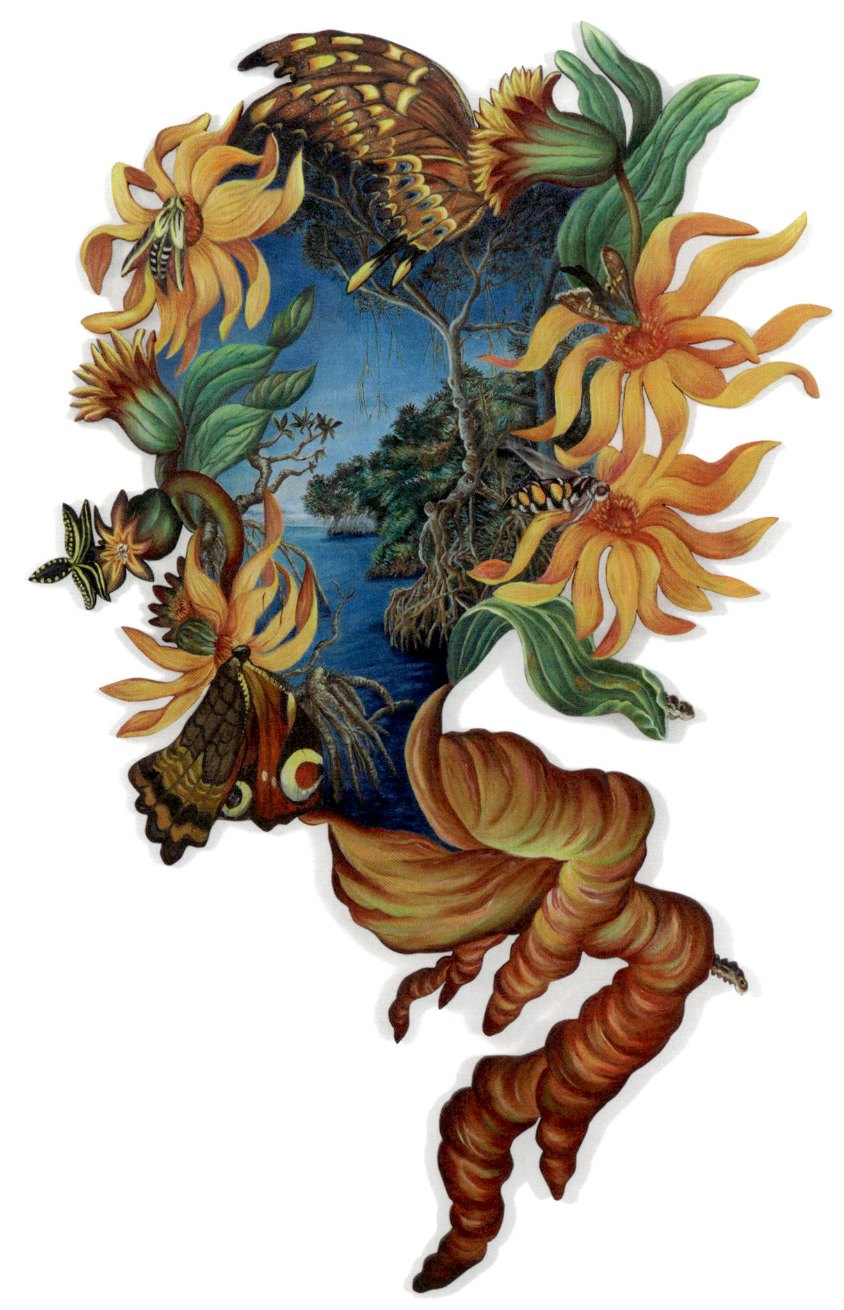

ALEXA KLEINBARD, *Arnica* from the series *REMEDIES*, 2003–2008. Oil on birchwood, 45 1/2 x 36 inches (115.6 cm x 91.4). Collection of Frank and Peper Willis. © Alexa Kleinbard. Photo by Jon Nalon.

Alexa Kleinbard

BORN IN ABINGTON, PENNSYLVANIA, 1952

Mother Nature ruled my growing up. Dad's fruit trees and flower gardens introduced me to pollinators, ants, beetles, rabbits, birds, and lighting bugs. Flower Fairies, poems about plants, and *The Jungle Book* inspired dreams of living in the forest. Learning to sew at ten, I cut out plant and animal shapes from fabric, sewing them onto patterned backgrounds, which became my first "natural world" artworks. Tree climbing inspired drawings of "far away" and bird's-eye views. After crossing the country camping and hiking in national parks, I became visually immersed in nature and her inhabitants.

In 1982, I was almost killed in a car accident—the car landed upside down on top of me. This close call intensified my thoughts on how our earth was having its own close call. Soon my work expanded into visual narratives concerning humankind's unstoppable appetite for natural materials…to build everything with.

I eventually began creating shaped paintings that have painted portals in their centers, which offer a view into worlds of beauty that might likely be done in by humankind. Their rhythmic root systems were inspired by music and dance, and highlight the important role this part of the plant plays in significantly nourishing the entire plant community and shared ecosystem. These early shaped paintings of plants have titles such as *Talking Leaves*, *Native Endangered Plants of Florida*, *Thistles*, and *Aphrodisiacs*. I have continued creating drawings and paintings that depict the medicinal native plants I have found growing wild in North Florida, Georgia, and the Carolinas in the series *REMEDIES*. This series

was inspired by my long-term exploration of folklore and medicinal recipes
from Indigenous peoples, of the physical and psychological healing properties that
plants have given generously throughout time and which must be protected.
Plants sustain all living things, their bloodlines run through everything. I begin with
graphite drawings, later transferring the line to gessoed birchwood, which I cut
into silhouettes of the healing plants with all their pollinators looking into a portal
of endangered wetlands they depend on to sustain them. These works, each named
after the individual plant, highlight the plant's habitat, the native animals around
it, and its unique properties: arnica, for example, is miraculous at reducing bruising;
senna helps with digestion; mayapple is helpful for warts and stomach issues;
and passionflower can be used as a sedative and to induce sleep. Our Georgia
mountain land, which has been declared an Appalachian Botanical Sanctuary
because of its abundance of rare native plants, has also become a "field library"
for me to draw from.

Many natural healers have been women. Observing how Mother Nature takes
care of us humans, we now know that a woman's loving touch is needed to take
care of our earth. Women, as primary caretakers, originally used spiderwebs to
pack wounds and stop bleeding. They watched birds make their nests using healing
herbs to keep their chicks healthy, so they started using herbs to keep away harmful
pests. My art will continue to bridge the mysterious worlds of nature and humans
while showing more and more what, and why, we must protect our only Garden of
Life from humankind's greedy encroachment of the earth's surface and oceans.

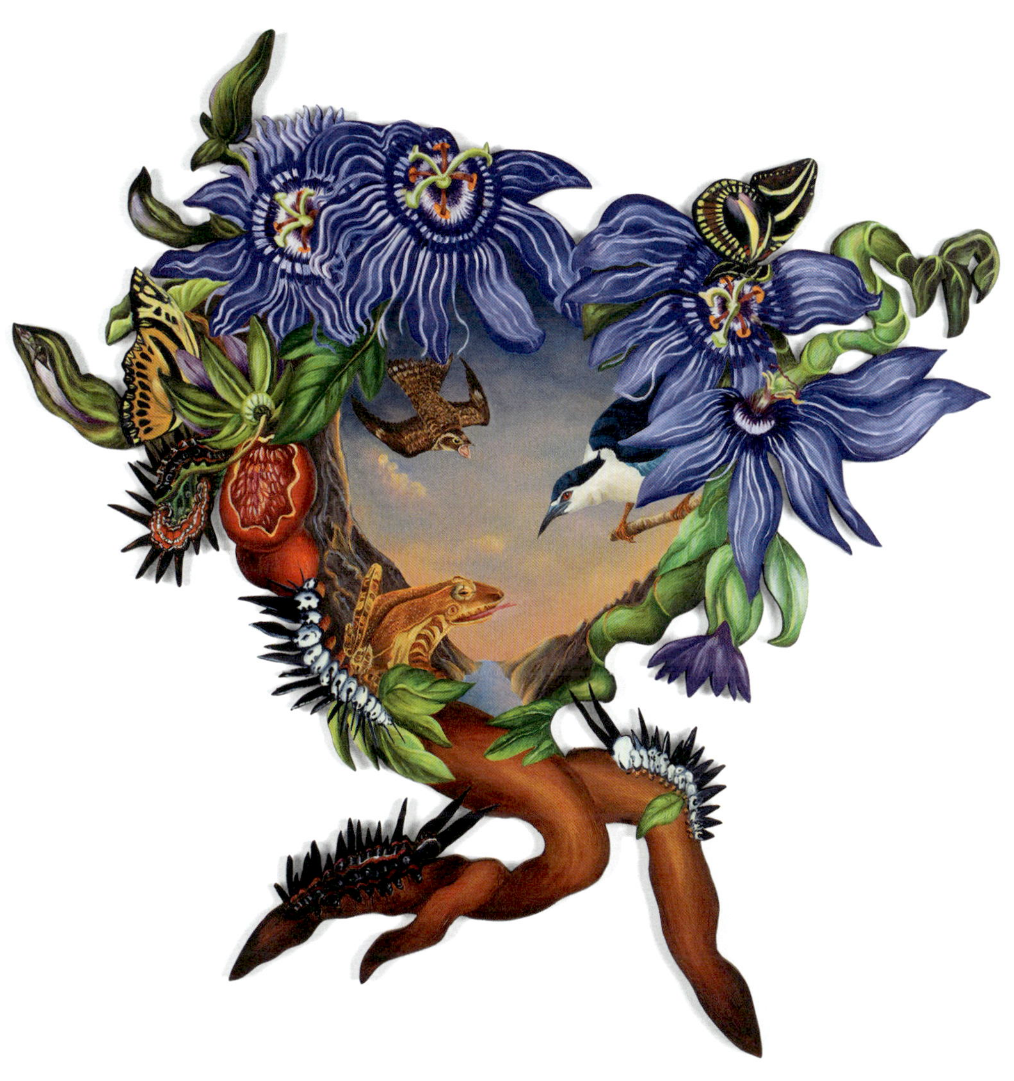

ALEXA KLEINBARD, *Passion Flower* from the series *REMEDIES*, 2003–2008. Oil on birchwood, 44 1/2 x 33 inches (113 x 83.8 cm). Courtesy of the artist. © Alexa Kleinbard. Photo by Jon Nalon.

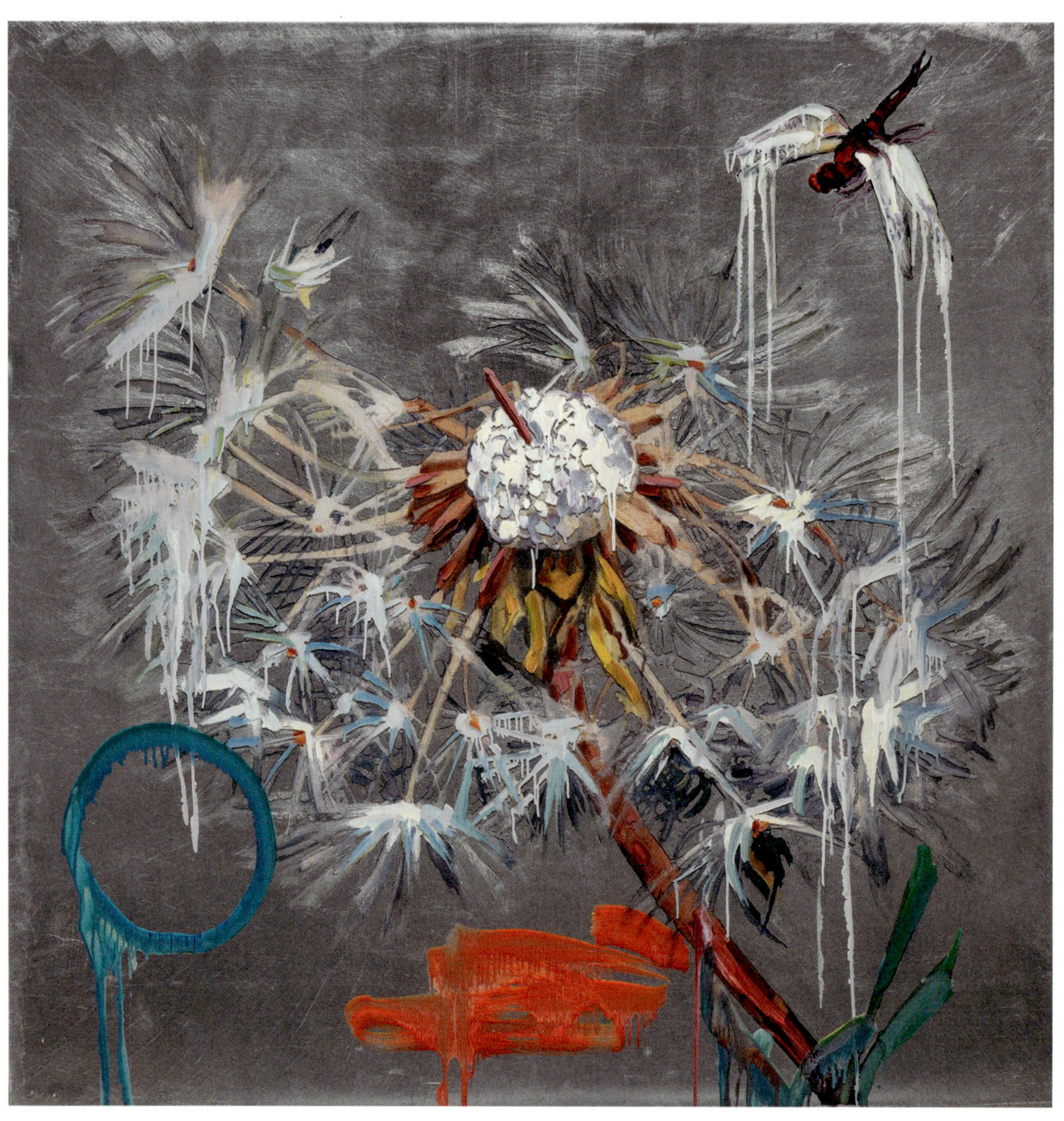

HUNG LIU, *Dandelion with Red Dragonfly (silver)*, 2020. Mixed media, 48 x 48 inches (121.9 x 121.9 cm). Collection of the Nasher Museum of Art at Duke University, Durham, North Carolina. Museum purchase, 2021.21.1. © Estate of Hung Liu. Photo by Peter Paul Geoffrion.

Hung Liu

BORN IN CHANGCHUN, CHINA, 1948; DIED 2021

Years ago, when my husband and I were on a road trip in the US, I found so many dandelions—they remind me of my childhood. I grew up in China. During childhood, we called dandelions "little parachutes" because they fly and land somewhere. But here, I heard that people blow the dandelion seeds away and make a wish.

The one thing that amazed me is they're everywhere. From East to West, from different continents, people would send me pictures of dandelions. In Europe, and actually last night, I took a picture at dusk of a dandelion in New Jersey. To me it's about the memory, but also dandelions are really migrant seeds; like a migration, they fly away, take their chance, they're actually other babies that grow up…but the seeds are babies at the same time, and they contain a future, and they depend on where they're going to land, and the next generation. They're everywhere and you can never kill them… I love them because they're not even flowers, they're just weeds, and they're resilient. I love them; they're so beautiful. And each one is so different. I love them even if they've lost a lot of seeds. Sometimes there is just one seed left, hanging there waiting to fly away, so I think it's about hope, let's say the hope of seeds. And also the possibility of taking a chance.[1]

> —Excerpt from a 2021 video interview, courtesy
> of Nancy Hoffman Gallery, New York, 2021.

1 Transcript has been edited for clarity and condensed. Video of the full interview available here: https://vimeo.com/576871949.

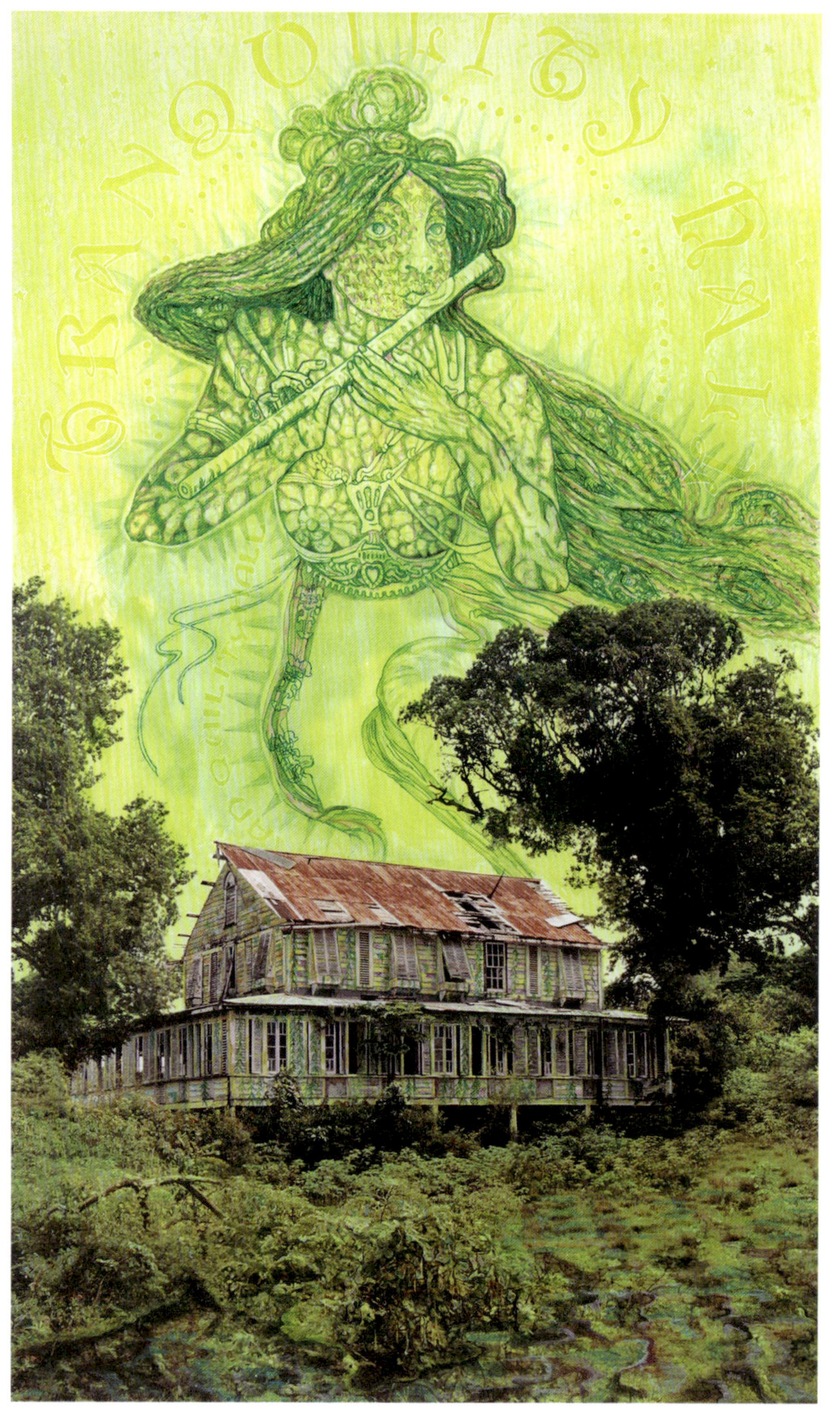

Hew Locke

BORN IN EDINBURGH, UNITED KINGDOM, 1959

Many countries are at risk of major flooding due to global warming—Guyana is one of them. Its agricultural coastal strip covers 10% of the land, houses 90% of the population, and is on average one meter (approximately three feet) below sea level. During the early colonial period this land was reclaimed by the Dutch, who used slave labor to build a nation-spanning seawall, back-dam, and canal system. As a child I lived right next to the seawall in Guyana's capital, Georgetown, a city crisscrossed by canals, drainage ditches, and sluice gates. When it rained heavily we prayed for a flood big enough to get a day off school—today the floods are more frequent.

When I was painting *Mosquito Hall*, I suddenly realized that the vague shapes in the distance were sandbags, stacked up because the seawall had been breached by high tides. For many years I have been obsessed with Guyanese vernacular wooden architecture. These building are rotting and fast disappearing. As a child I would dream of being rich enough to live in one of the big plantation houses, so this body of work has an air of nostalgia for me. Living as I do in Britain the past has literally become a foreign country, and these houses the ghosts of my memory. The flooded houses in my images are then both floods of nostalgia and a metaphor for the washing away of my memories.

Mosquito Hall and *Tranquility Hall* are named after the villages where these houses are situated. They remind me of art nouveau posters I saw in old houses when I was a child. *Mosquito Hall* depicts a mixed-race woman holding her child. We can speculate who the baby's father is. I was thinking of the racial hierarchies

HEW LOCKE, *Tranquility Hall*, 2013. Acrylic on chromogenic print, 83 $^7/_8$ x 49 $^3/_4$ inches (213 x 126.4 cm). Courtesy of the artist, Hales Gallery, and P•P•O•W. © Hew Locke. All Rights Reserved, DACS 2023.

existing at this time. She is surrounded by pre-Columbian figures and memento mori skeletons. The flute player in *Tranquility Hall* will remind Guyanese of the ghost story *My Bones and My Flute* by Edgar Mittelholzer, set in the bush and harking back to the 1763 slave rebellion.

The Bush is what we call the vast jungle hinterland of Guyana, a place the majority of the population never visits. We turn our backs on this intimidating, often impenetrable forest, and look out to the sea instead. Still, the bush is an ever-abiding presence in our folklore, legends, and culture. In my works such as *Black Queen*, I have been inspired by the undergrowth—the seething sea of tiny life that exists under our feet in the tropics. Insects, plants, reptiles—plants and animals I know only by their local names—such as crapau (toad), sherriga (crab), sword trees, married man pork (basil), white lady guavas, labba, youri (possum), banga mary (fish), Follow me (wasps), baby pumpkin, turpentine mangoes, chicken foot (heliconia flower), tiger-cat (jaguar), comoudi (anaconda)…

Walter Raleigh believed El Dorado was situated in Guyana, and like all small boys I was fascinated by the myth of golden riches and civilizations in the bush. My grandfather was what we call a Pork Knocker for a time—abandoning his family on the coast to travel into the bush to prospect for gold, like many adventurous men did and still do. Guyana has now found El Dorado, but it is offshore black gold. From one of the poorest countries in the world, it is expected to become one of the richest per capita. Ironically some of this fossil fuel–derived wealth will be needed to prop up the sea defenses against global warming.

In my paintings I often trying to recreate a particular acid green or yellow that generates a mood or feeling I remember from my childhood, one of tropical humidity or light. The color of the air itself when it has a humid stifling intensity. This color I'm trying to grasp is always just out of reach, a flash you can sometimes just catch from the corner of your eye. A past you can never go back to, that for me is embodied in this color.

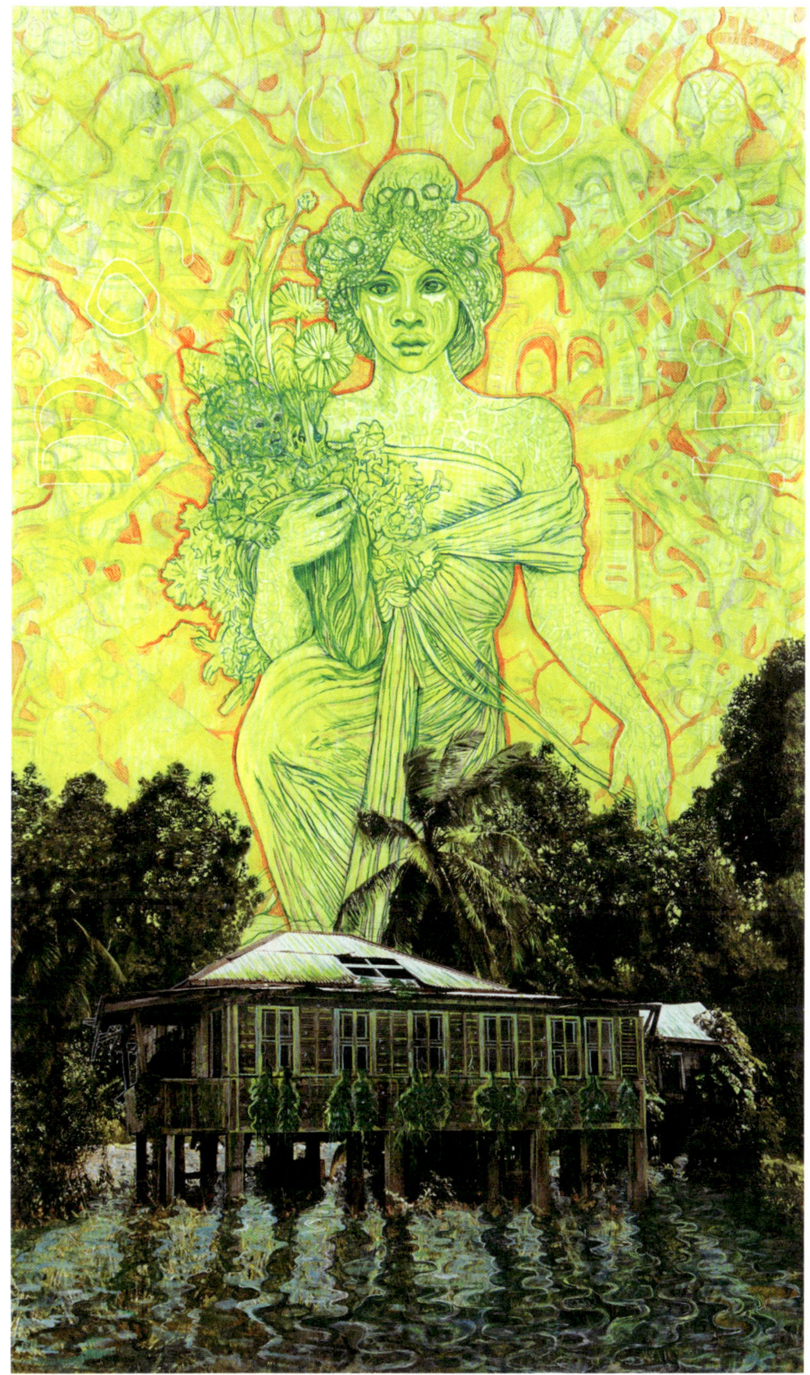

HEW LOCKE, *Mosquito Hall*, 2013. Acrylic on chromogenic print, 83 7/8 x 49 3/4 inches (213 x 126.4 cm). Collection of the Nasher Museum of Art at Duke University, Durham, North Carolina. Museum purchase, 2022.22.1. © Hew Locke. All Rights Reserved, DACS 2023. Courtesy of the artist, Hales Gallery, and P•P•O•W.

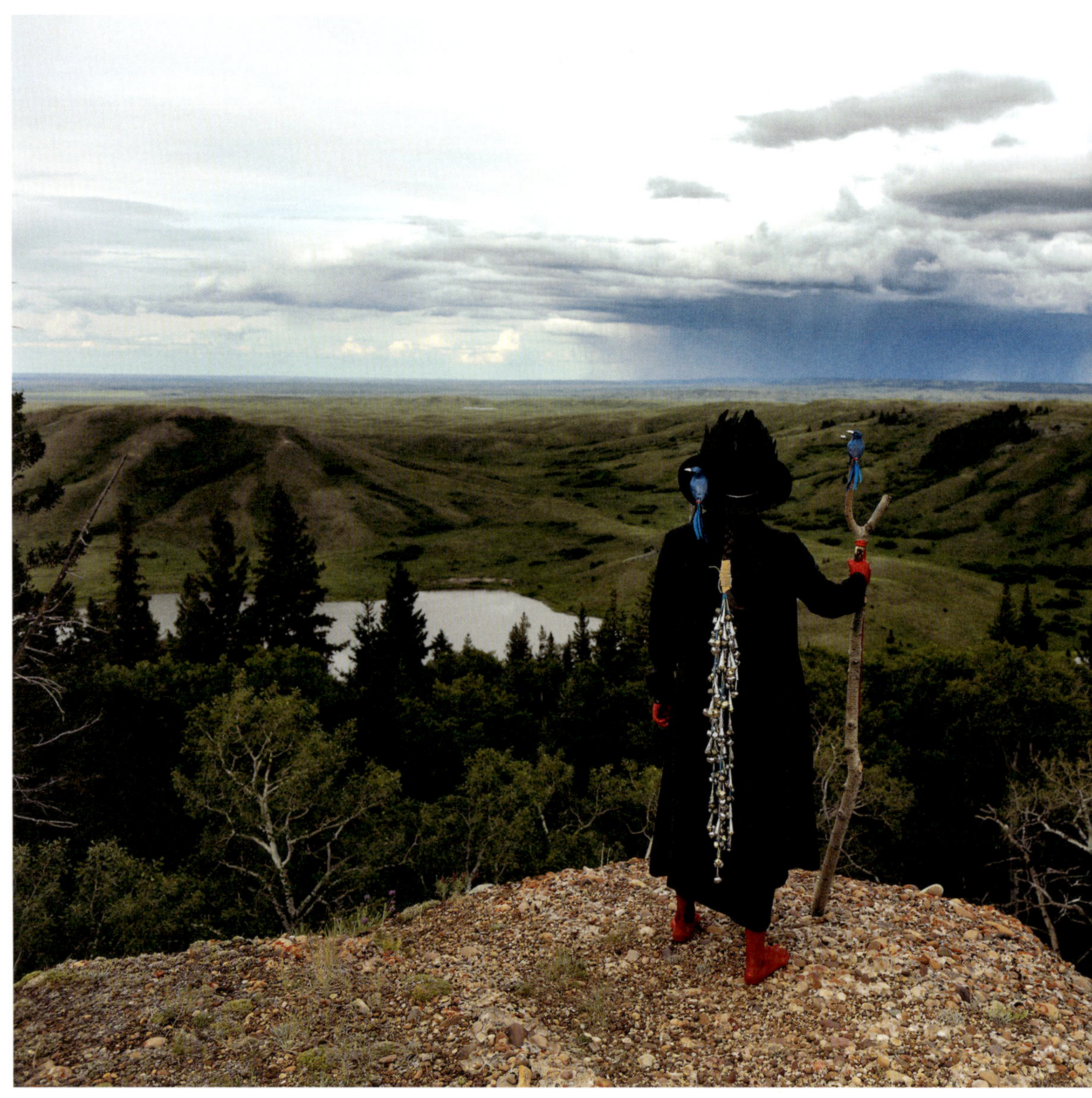

MERYL MCMASTER, *My Destiny is Entwined With Yours* from the series *As Immense as the Sky*, 2019. Chromogenic print mounted on aluminum composite panel, 40 x 60 inches (101.6 x 152.4 cm). Courtesy of the artist and Stephen Bulger Gallery and Pierre-François Ouellette art contemporain. © Meryl McMaster.

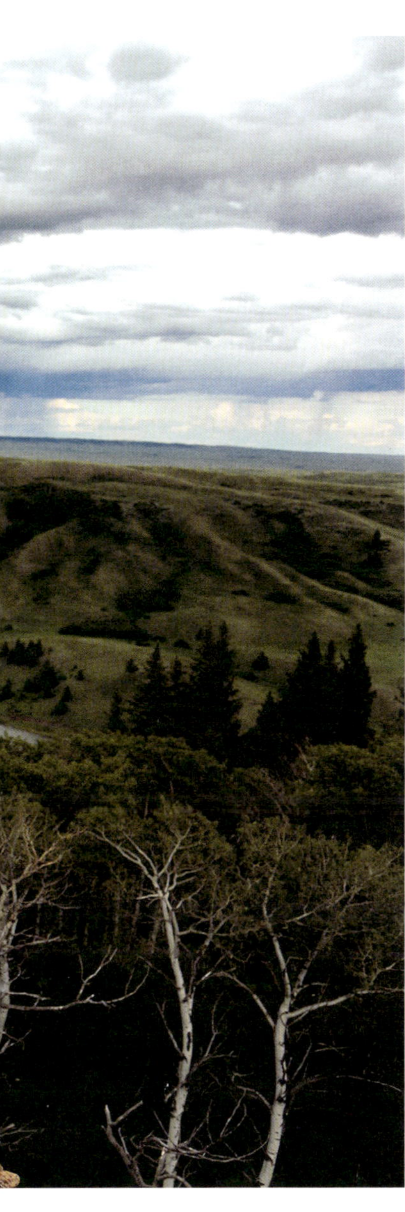

Meryl McMaster

PLAINS CREE/SIKSIKA NATION, BORN IN OTTAWA,
CANADA, 1988

I gave birth to my daughter in 2020. Immediately following her birth, we introduced her to the world with a private ceremony, in much the same way my parents did for me. To the four directions, to the earth and sky, everything as witness. It is a gesture of being in the world, and the world becoming part of us, activating our relationship to the environment. This connection with and reverence for the natural world has always been with me. Eventually I found a way of incorporating it into my art practice.

All throughout my youth, I have had experiences that strengthened this relationship to nature. Whether it was traveling and living for weeks at a time camping, hiking, canoeing, or reforesting, these have become the experiences I've had in the many traditional territories of Indigenous peoples across the Americas. Today, my home is located steps from a vast forest. All this and more is what becomes me.

I acknowledge that there are many truths in the land. Whether these are the received stories from ancient times, known historical events or those I've personally lived through, I have found ways of working them into my photography. Part of my ancestry originates from the northern end of the Great Plains. In the two works in this exhibition,

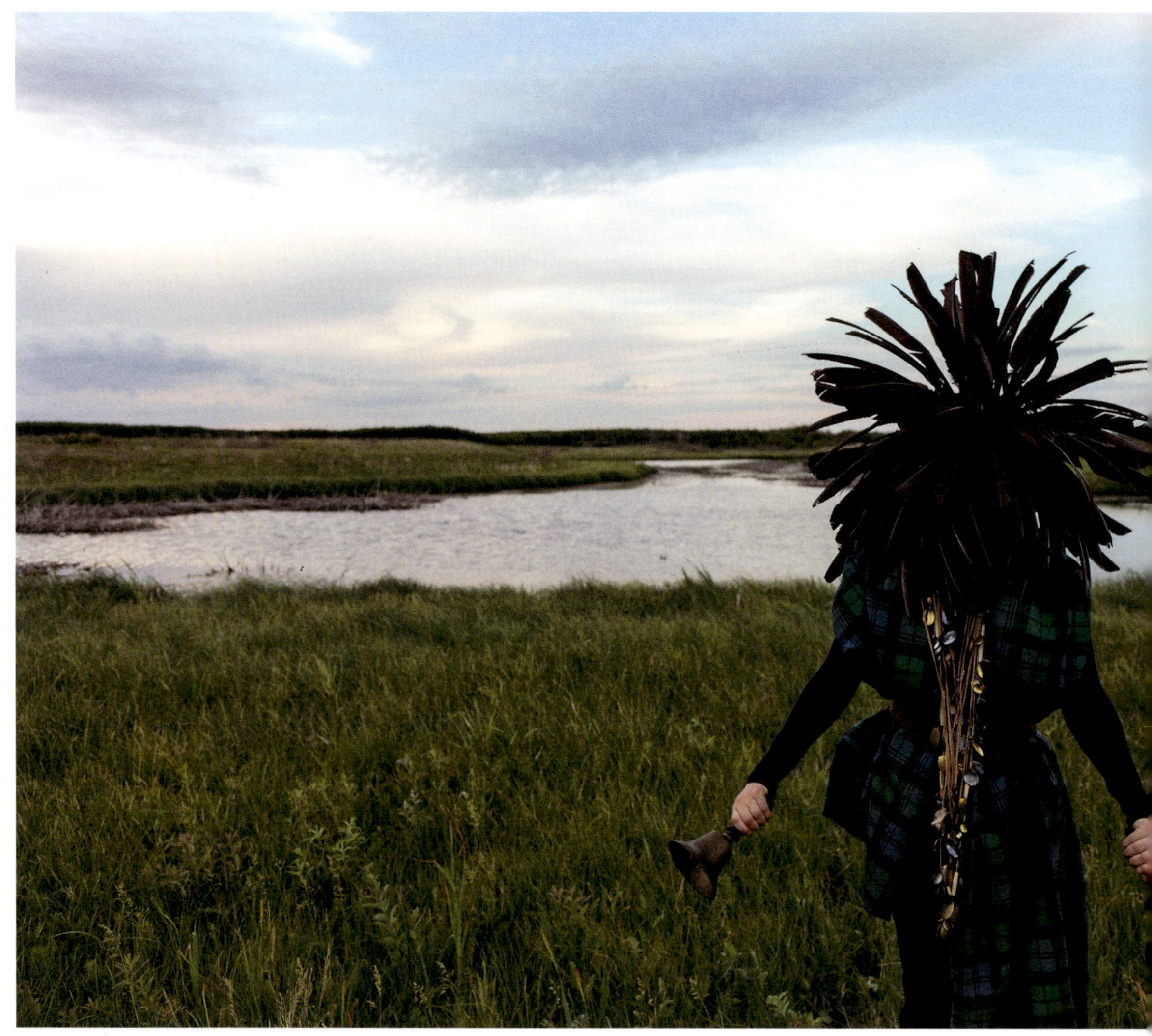

I used the Saskatchewan landscape. In *My Destiny is Entwined With Yours*, a lone figure looks out from the highest point on the Prairies that was left untouched by the Ice Age. This extraordinary ancestral place holds a network of hunting and gathering areas as well as sacred sites. In the far-off distance a cloud bursts, sending water down upon a parched earth. This phenomenon of the earth saturated with life-giving waters is a stunning sight. In *From a Still Unquiet Place*, a feather-bonneted figure rings bells into the landscape, summoning a connection to the history and traditions of this place, momentarily interrupting the natural rhythms surrounding the family home.

The landscapes I work with are immense time capsules of buried knowledge and stories. So how can I know a fragment? I know it'll take a lifetime for me to understand the many teachings of *okâwîmâwaskiy* (mother of all earth). With each passing year I continue to recall and appreciate the wanderings I've had across the many landscapes, journeys that will eventually become realized in my work. I feel that as I continue seeking out the places of ancestral life and knowledge, I am continually enriched.

When I was introduced to the world by my parents through a ceremony, I became part of the world as witness and that invested me with an immense moral responsibility to ensure that I leave my daughter with the same reverence for the earth that was passed on to me.

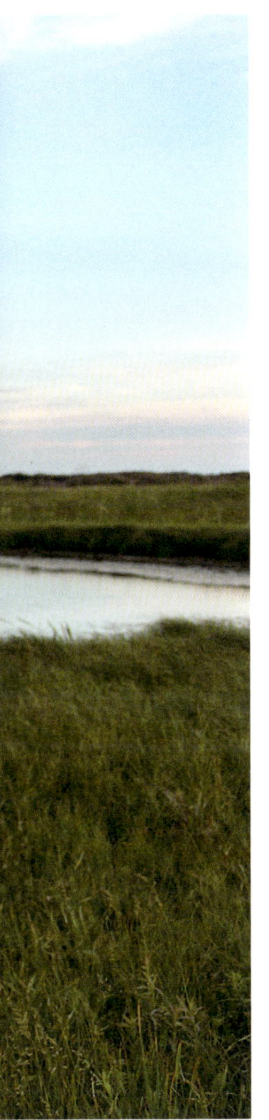

MERYL MCMASTER, *From a Still Unquiet Place* from the series *As Immense as the Sky*, 2019. Chromogenic print mounted on aluminum composite panel, 40 x 60 inches (101.6 x 152.4 cm). Courtesy of the artist and Stephen Bulger Gallery and Pierre-François Ouellette art contemporain. © Meryl McMaster.

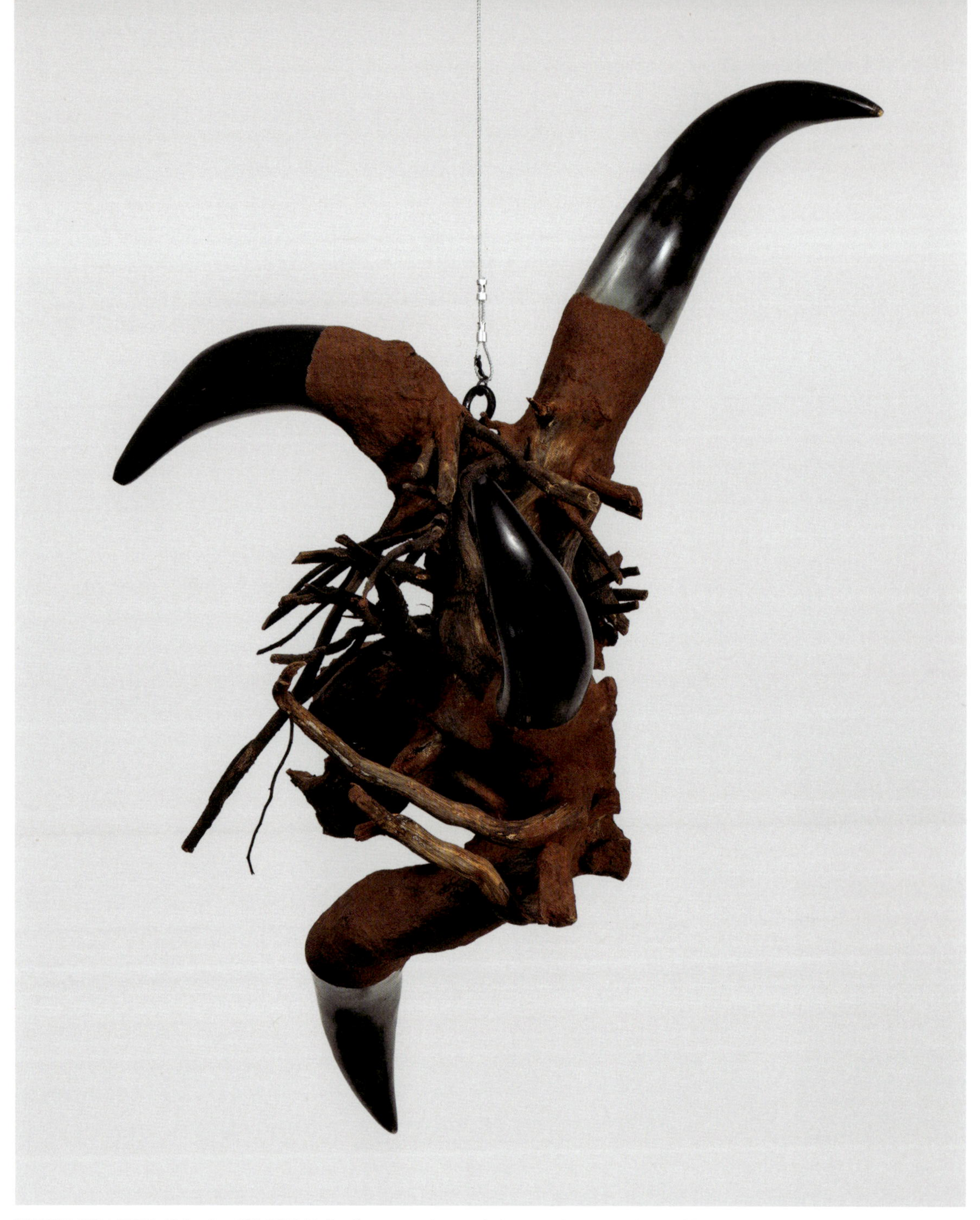

WANGECHI MUTU, *Flying Root IV*, 2017. Red soil, paper pulp, wood glue, wood, and cow horns; 23 x 16 x 17 inches (58.4 x 40.6 x 43.2 cm). Courtesy of the artist and Gladstone Gallery. © Wangechi Mutu.

Wangechi Mutu

BORN IN NAIROBI, KENYA, 1972

Land and earth, sea and air are unownable, because they are in essence ALL of us, as a whole. Indivisible and unownable. The oldest mother, home, and the original womb. There's no way they can be given, sold, or leased, because they are the sum of us all. We are the Land, and quite simply, our earth is us.

> [In the eighteenth and early nineteenth centuries there was a Kenyan Sage, from the Gikuyu people, named] Mugo wa Kibiru or Chege (Cege) wa Kibiru. His name "Mugo" means "a healer." Chege's prophecies were that there would come a race of people whose skin complexion would resemble a small pale-colored frog that lives in water (kiengere), and one would be able to see their blood flowing under their skins just like the frog.[1]

Our stories, our songs, our poems, our carvings and drawings, our sculptures, all of our gods and our ghosts, all of our machines and our theories, all our intelligences come from the earth. An imbalance and injustice of unbelievable proportions is causing us to violate our earth; kill, assault, rape, torture, and starve multitudes of humans; and produce fantasies of superiority in the name of civilization and cultivation. We fail our consciousness, live on fear and disease, forgetting that our cures, our bodies, our nutrition, come from this one thing, from this amniotic fluid of bountiful balance of land and of sea.

> [Chege was legendary for his accurate prophecies. The great Sage] predicted with astonishing accuracy that there would be a famine in Kikuyu-land that would exterminate much of the tribe right before the arrival of these pale-colored strangers or foreigners [and that the Kikuyus would be taken over by these strangers,] but that [it] would end after many years (sixty-eight years). Chege predicted that a giant [Mugumo] fig tree five meters in diameter located in Thika, north of Nairobi, would wither and die by the day Kenya gained independence.[2]

We continue to move away from understanding the land, from understanding original wisdoms, and from our home. All inhabitants of Earth, all the animals, birds, lizards, insects, all manner of visible and nearly invisible organisms are capable of hearing and speaking to one another. But we keep moving away.

Surely, we have an original mother tongue. The tongue of origin, like a fat pink coral found inside the mouth of the original ocean language.

The exhilaration and stimulation that city life affords us, the voices, bodies, ideas, lightning bolting everywhere between tall steel buildings and highways, distance us from soil and sky, and obscure and shatter the view of Earth's surface, of horizon, of ocean, and of land. Tongue-tied, ears clogged with vehicle sounds, tweets, explosives, machine language, and a drone of disenchantment.

> [The Mugumo tree,] was regarded as sacred by the Kikuyus; even the British administrators/colonialists took the prophecy very seriously, [and] tended to and reinforced the fig tree, [building] an iron ring around it to prevent it from falling. Shortly before Kenya gained independence from the British, the fig tree was struck by lightning, and began to wither rapidly. On 12th December 1963, when Kenya officially became an independent state, the tree had decayed and died, thereby fulfilling Chege wa Kibiru's prophecy over a century earlier. [3]

Land will never belong to those who create countries and nations, territories, or reserves.

The earth is not ours and never will be. The earth is us and ever will be.

1 "Kikuyu History: Mugo wa Kibiru, The Kikuyu Seer," *Discover Africa Blog*, February 27, 2021, https://www.discoverafricablog.com/mugo-wa-kibiru-the-kikuyu-seer.

2 "Kikuyu History," *Discover Africa Blog*.

3 "Kikuyu History," *Discover Africa Blog*.

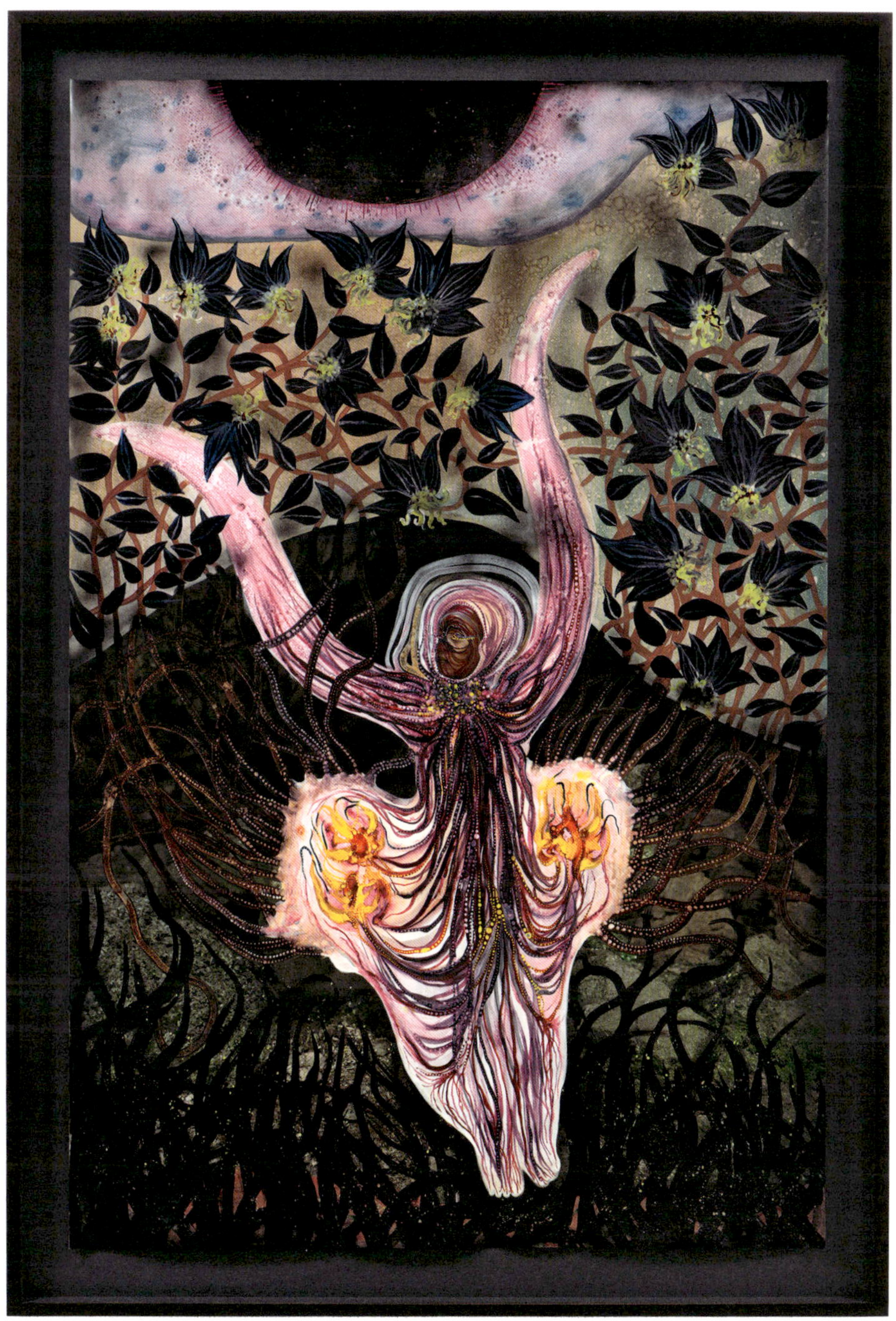

WANGECHI MUTU, *Subterranea Flourish*, 2021. Ink and emulsion paint on photographic print, 72 x 48 inches (182.9 x 121.9 cm). Private collection, California. © Wangechi Mutu.

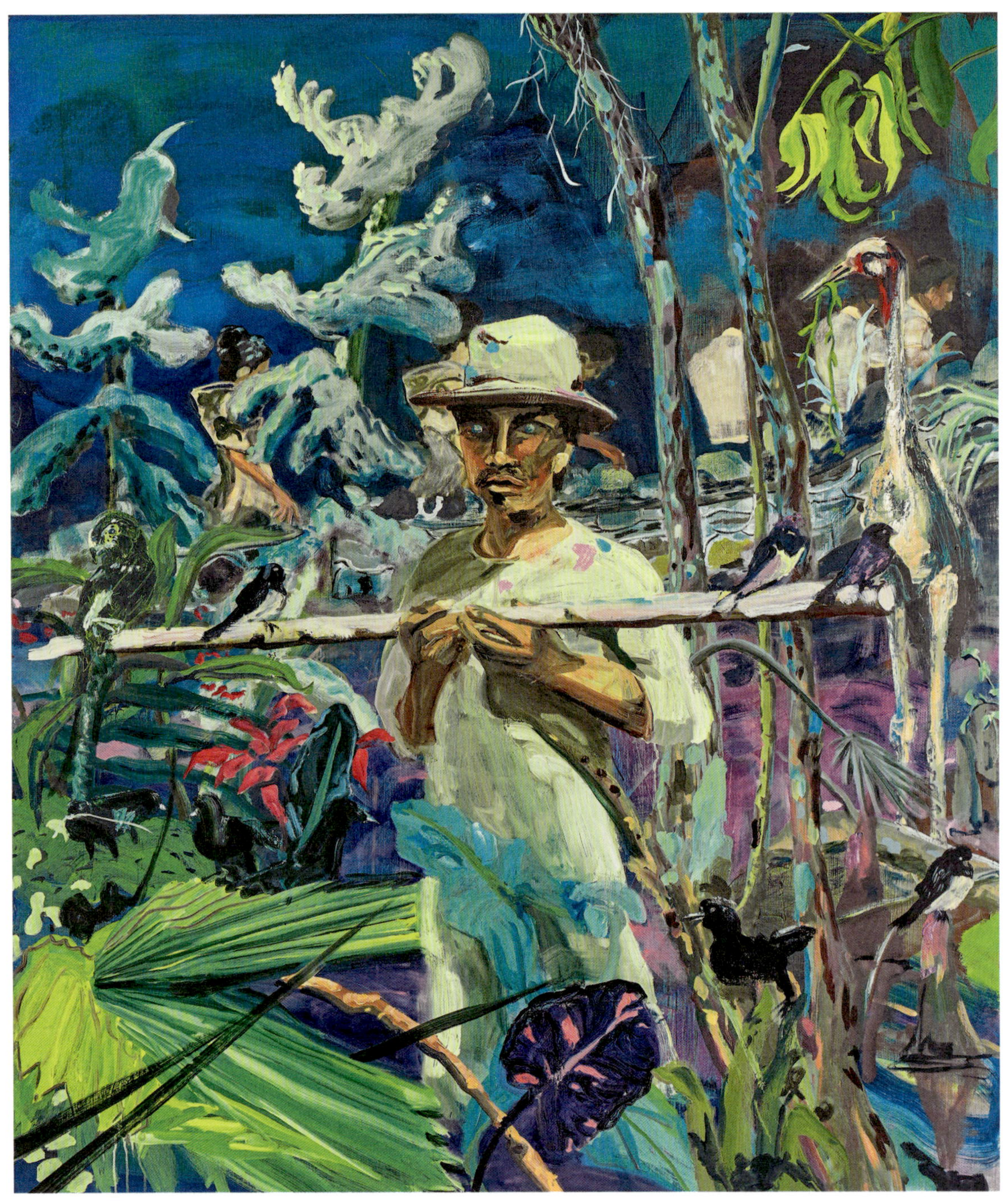

MAIA CRUZ PALILEO, *Conference of the Birds*, 2019. Oil on linen, 60 x 52 inches (152.4 x 132.1 cm). Private collection, courtesy Monique Meloche Gallery. © Maia Cruz Palileo. Courtesy of the artist and Monique Meloche Gallery.

Maia Cruz Palileo

BORN IN CHICAGO, ILLINOIS, 1979

Driving through the mountains at night, Tita Cherry whispers the story of Maria Makiling, a land goddess who lives in the mountains. Tito Danny, when he babysits, warns of *duendes*, spirits that come out at night in order to keep us home after dark. When we came in from playing outside in the summer, mom would smell our sunbaked heads and say, *"Amoy araw*, you smell like the sun," a poetic way of saying, "You stink, go take a bath." When she passed away, I dreamt of her warm hands in the middle of the ocean.

It is mid-August, and I am at the Newberry Library in Chicago. In the reading room, an archival box of photographs awaits my attention. Fifty photos per box, mounted on board and wrapped in plastic. A man stands in the middle of a group, butchering an animal from a hunt. He looks off to the side, beyond the frame. Peering through a magnifying glass, I draw his face, hat, and torso. I unfold a small triptych of photographs, mounted, taped together, and tri-folded like a letter. It is a panorama of a river. Shrubs and rocks pepper the shore, and trees bulge and poke into the sky. Tiny bathers dot the river. On the shore, a solitary figure stands, back turned to the viewer, looking beyond the edges of the picture at what we cannot see: longing and desire. These photographs provide a glimpse of the plants, rivers, mountains, animals, skies, terraces, forests, and people of my family's homeland. This is what I came here to see, albeit through the lens of the American colonial camera.

On the side of the road, Dad bends over a tiny plant and calls to me. He wants to show me something. The leaves are long and oval shaped, attached to the stem perpendicularly, getting smaller toward the tip. He gently brushes a leaf with his finger. A moment later, the plant begins to close. In pairs, leaves rise and join together like hands in prayer. What was the surface of the leaves a moment ago has become the plant's carefully guarded inside. Dad explains, "Back home we call this plant *makahiya* because it is shy."

Multiple paintings in different stages line the walls in my studio. I am waiting, but I don't know what I am waiting for. The hardest part of painting is starting. No. The hardest part is returning. Stay. I want the surface of the water in this painting to look wet. Mix paint with stand oil, lay the canvas flat, apply the paint, and leave it to dry for the next ten days. Sometimes a painting starts with a general idea, like water or spring. Once the color hits the surface, the painting suddenly, and at times awkwardly, begins to slip away. My job is to follow it, to look and listen, gently brush until the painting shyly clasps shut, frozen in prayer.

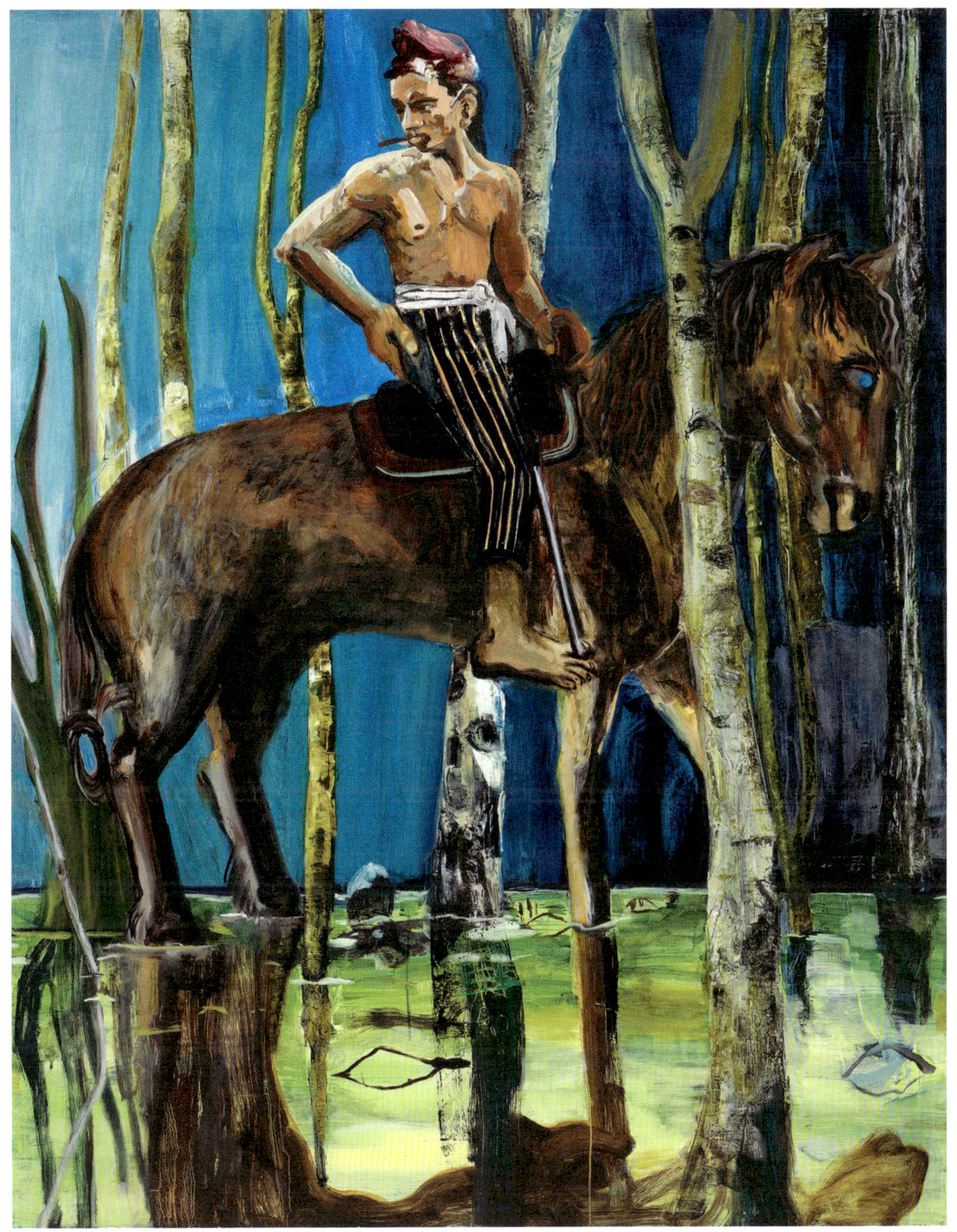

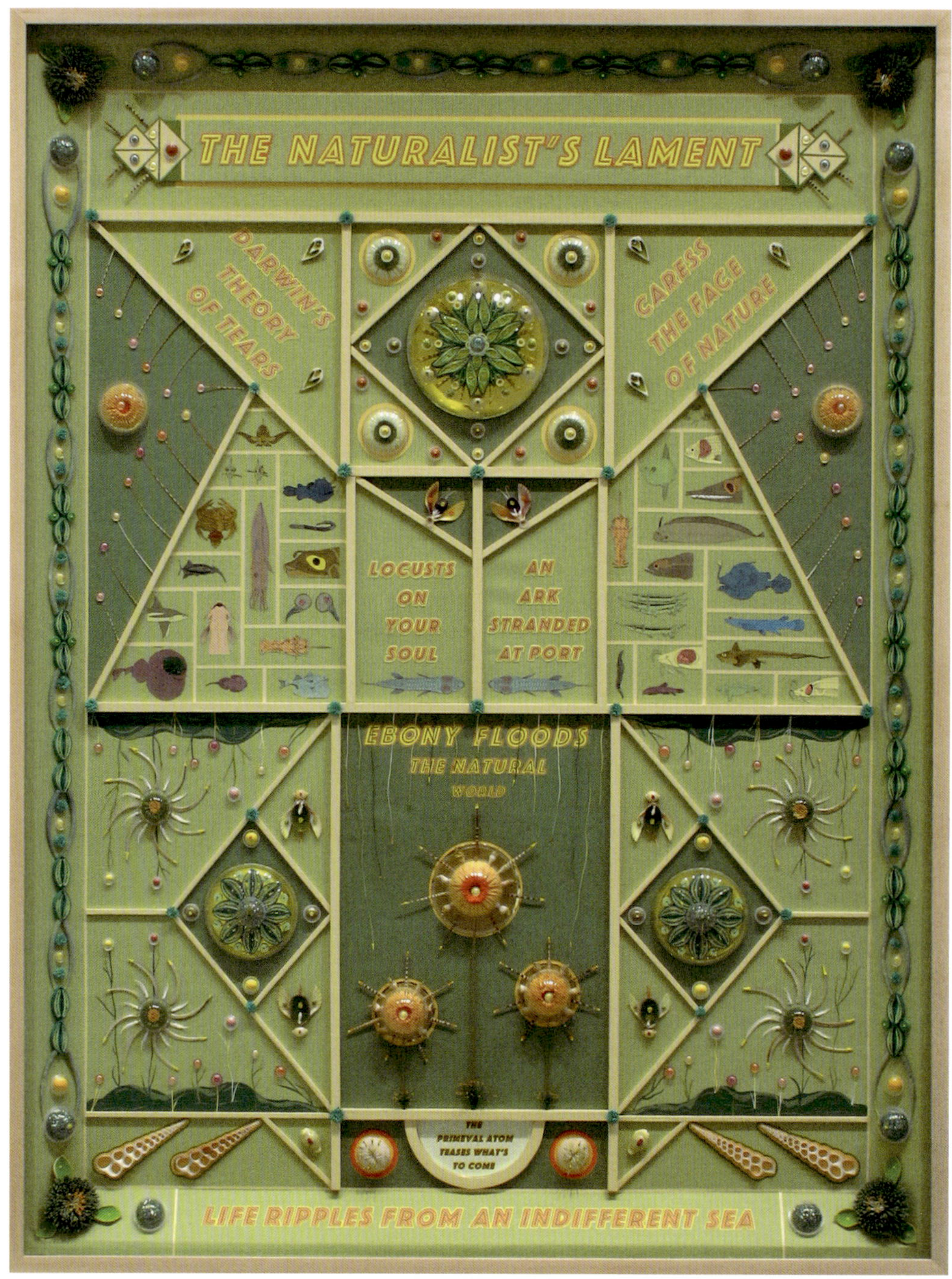

DARIO ROBLETO, *The Naturalist's Lament,* 2017. Cut paper, various cut and polished seashells, urchin spines, green tusks, squilla claws, mushroom coral, colored powder pigments and beads, colored crushed glass and wire, plastic domes, prints on paper, colored and mirrored Plexiglas, foam core, glue, and frame; 51 $^7/_{16}$ x 39 $^1/_4$ x 3 $^1/_2$ inches (130.7 x 99.7 x 8.9 cm). Courtesy of the artist. © Dario Robleto.

Dario Robleto

BORN IN SAN ANTONIO, TEXAS, 1972

In the summer of 2007, I touched a glacier older than the written word. At least seven thousand years ago, in an area of the globe we now call Montana, the Grinnell Glacier wrapped its glorious chill across hundreds of acres of mountain ranges. It is a wonder to behold, the embodiment of geologic processes tipping into the human domains of poetry, awe, and empathy—it is impossible not to feel something for this timeworn behemoth. Compressing over time, the gentle impacts of innumerable snowflakes accumulated in mass, metamorphosing into ice as hard as stone and carrying the power to sculpt the Earth into new configurations. Give anything enough time, it seemed to be saying, and unforeseen transformation is possible; we can change our ways.

I stood on this ancient ice with Dan Fagre, a research ecologist with the United States Geological Survey. As I would later learn, Dan is also known as a "glaciologist," the only disciplinary category that can provoke some envy from my beloved title of "artist." It is a term reflective of the rise of modern science and its perpetual sequestering of knowledge into more specialized fields of study. But, as I would soon realize, to be a glaciologist today is to be something much older—older than science, the written word, or art. To be a glaciologist today is to be a mourner.

I listened to Dan with great interest, eager to understand the science of glacial formations and their impacts on geological features, freshwater supply, and the plant and animal life enabled through their cyclical behavior. But this is glacial science with a once reasonable assumption: glaciers will continue to exist for millennia. As I asked more questions, as he showed me the stunning retreat of this glacier's mass over a century of photographs, it was apparent Dan carried other observations, too. Dan, I would argue, is part of something entirely new on Earth: an ever-growing category of scientists who, mid-career, must enfold the staggering loss and possible extinction of their chosen subject into their science.

As a concept, "extinction" was only first scientifically embraced in the nineteenth century. It seemed unlikely that entire life-forms could simply vanish; or, to the religious-minded, that God would make such "mistakes." But with accumulating fossil evidence, Darwin's radical theory of evolution, and a growing sense of the actual age of the planet, the idea that life-forms, through natural processes, could meet a dead end slowly took hold.[1] But whatever the mechanisms, extinction was not a process anyone expected to see in real time. With time, though, humanity could not ignore its role in a once inconceivably abstract process, creating a profound new category of moral consequence: human-induced extinction.

Let's be clear about what this means. This new category of scientists is not like paleontologists, for example—scientists who have chosen to research extinct life-forms of the distant past. If fossil hunters have a sense of melancholy about this loss of life, it is removed from the moral morass of human behavior—this loss happened long ago. But Dan, and hundreds of ornithologists, entomologists, botanists, ichthyologists, dendrologists, and more, are witnessing, in real time, the threshold of *life as it currently exists* to *life as it once was*. And it is a process instigated, in growing ways, by the actions of fellow humans. How does one comprehend and articulate such grief and sorrow? How can one make sense of irrational behavior that risks the annihilation of one's species and the planet? Through logic and measurement, can science alone ever adequately voice what should also be a trial of our souls? Can ever more scientifically precise and worrisome environmental studies induce a reformulation of planetary stewardship and moral action? Science is essential, yes, but can it do it all?

If ever there was a call to arms for the sciences and humanities to find their way back to each other, then surely it was here on this melting cathedral of nature. Here we stood, an artist and a scientist, our footing unstable, but our grasp and shared heartbreak now fusing data and poetry into action. The naturalist's lament is the artist's lament: we must mourn with purpose. We must honestly look into an existential abyss of our making but not as an exercise in futility and hopelessness. We must look so that we might rekindle our love of *all* life, inventing new scientifically informed narratives and artworks about our obligation to life's continued survival.

1 See Paul Semonin, *American Monster: How the Nation's First Prehistoric Creature Became a Symbol of National Identity* (New York: NYU Press, 2000).

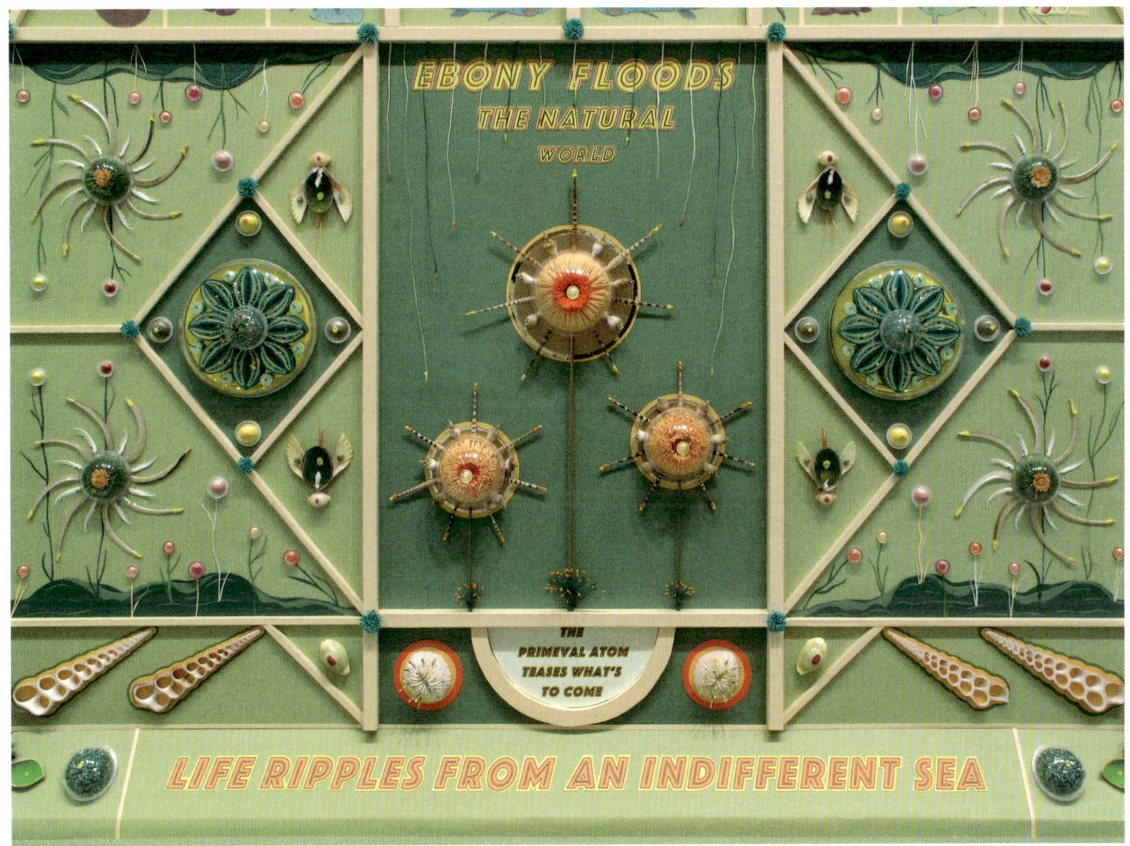

DARIO ROBLETO, *The Naturalist's Lament* (detail), 2017. Cut paper, various cut and polished seashells, urchin spines, green tusks, squilla claws, mushroom coral, colored powder pigments and beads, colored crushed glass and wire, plastic domes, prints on paper, colored and mirrored Plexiglas, foam core, glue, and frame; 51 7/16 x 39 1/4 x 3 1/2 inches (130.7 x 99.7 x 8.9 cm). Courtesy of the artist. © Dario Robleto.

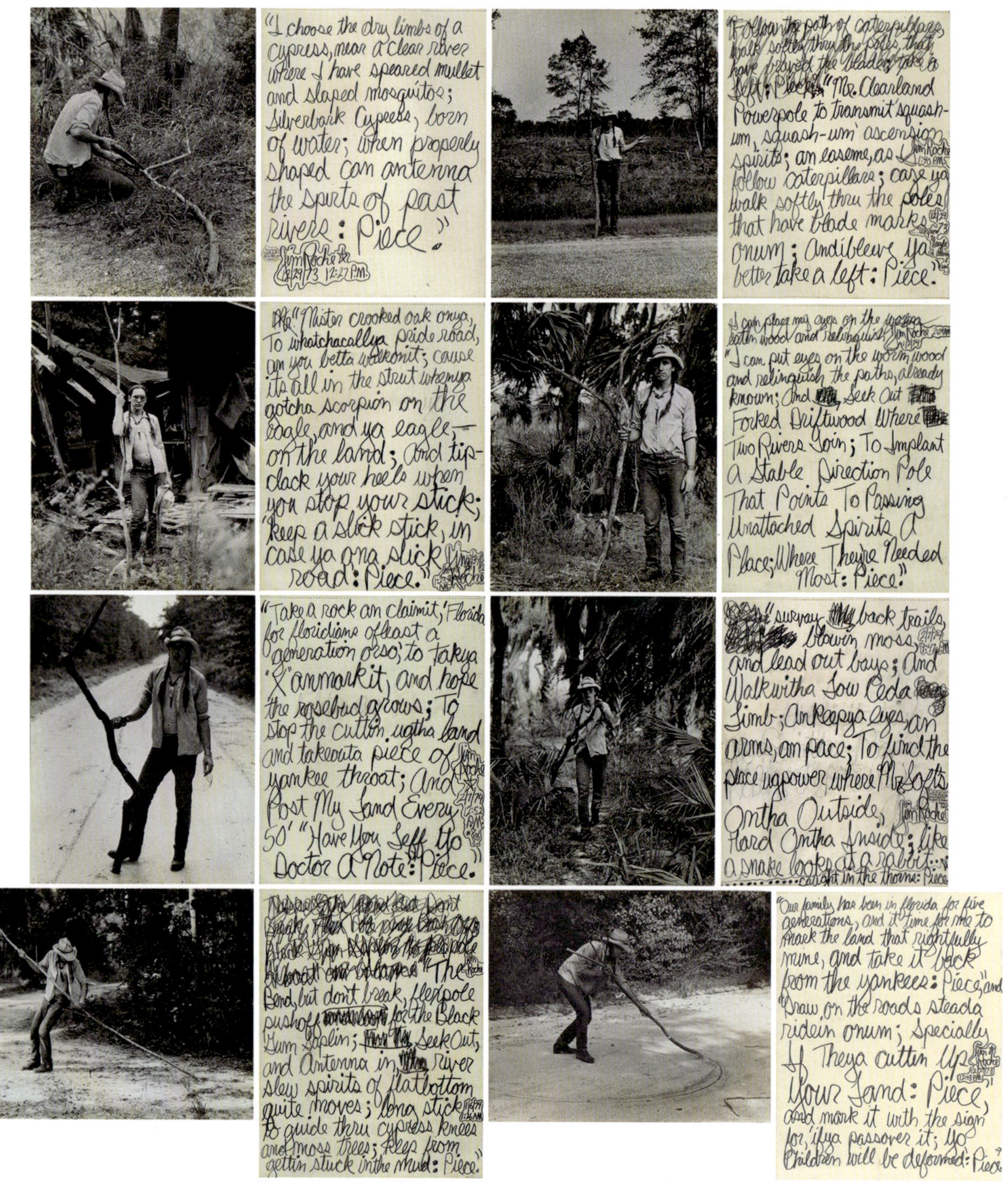

JIM ROCHE, *Return to Florida, All in My Background: Piece*, 1973–1974. Installation of eight pairs of gelatin silver prints and graphite works on paper, 20 x 16 inches (50.8 x 40.6 cm) (each panel). Collection of the Nasher Museum of Art at Duke University, Durham, North Carolina. Museum purchase and partial gift of Ken Rollins, President, Rollins Fine Art; 2016.19.1. © Jim Roche. Photos by Peter Paul Geoffrion and Brian Quinby.

Jim Roche

BORN IN JACKSON COUNTY, FLORIDA, 1943

As a child growing up in post–WWII Florida, my life was oriented around nature. I spent my summers cracking pecans, planting seeds and bulbs, picking fruit, fishing, hunting, camping, and making treehouses. Later on, I took a "camp-awhile" and then a "work-awhile" trip across the country, doing odd jobs, determined to see all of the splendor and natural beauty that our country had to offer. In 1966, I left home for grad school in Texas. I was reluctant to leave the lushness, biodiversity, crystal-clear springs, white sand beaches, and beautiful days in Florida, though I naively assumed it would remain a paradise forever.

It did not. When I returned to Florida in 1972, I was saddened, shocked, and angered that so many places were no longer there. The remote sinkholes, clear, fast-running rivers, ancient oaks and pines and all their diverse wildlife were now much harder to see. Jumping mullet fish, birds sweeping in large flocks, lightning bugs blinking in unison, dragonflies, huge spiders with patterned webs, bullfrogs singing and wild hogs searching, all suffering from industrialization and development. Everything was being killed, chased away, paved, cut or torn down.

New buildings seemed to be everywhere. Smaller Florida roads, once known for rare flowers found along their edges, were now being mowed on a regular basis. Large live oaks were being removed to make room for houses with plywood roofs, plastic plumbing, picture windows, and cropped grass yards. This was not "progress" to those of us who'd grown up there. I decided that

I should do some images of myself as a Floridian who had just
found out that the natural world was in danger of being destroyed
drastically fast. (I later would do a full-scale *Tree Grave Site* homage
to our natural world at Art Park in 1976.)

The text in the drawings of *Return to Florida, All in My Background:
Piece* are written in rhyme, which give titles to their accompanying
photos. The eight photo images are from different locations. I found
myself cutting saplings to point, walk, or draw in the sand with,
if needed. After choosing a special spot, I would voice out a phonic
rhyme, a kind of free form vocal "riff," to help arrive at the written
title, and feeling, of that physical spot, and what I absorbed there.

From back then to right now…I have put the natural world first, over
everything. So please consider that OUR EARTH HAS A FEVER!
IS MAN THE VIRUS?

"I choose the dry limbs of a cypress, near a clear river where I have speared mullet and slaped mosquitos; Silverbark Cypress, born of water; when properly shaped can antenna the spirts of past rivers: Piece."

Jim Roche
12/29/73 12:27 P.M.

JIM ROCHE, *Return to Florida, All in My Background: Piece* (detail), 1973–1974. Installation of eight pairs of gelatin silver prints and graphite works on paper, 20 x 16 inches (50.8 x 40.6 cm) (each panel). Collection of the Nasher Museum of Art at Duke University, Durham, North Carolina. Museum purchase and partial gift of Ken Rollins, President, Rollins Fine Art; 2016.19.1. © Jim Roche.

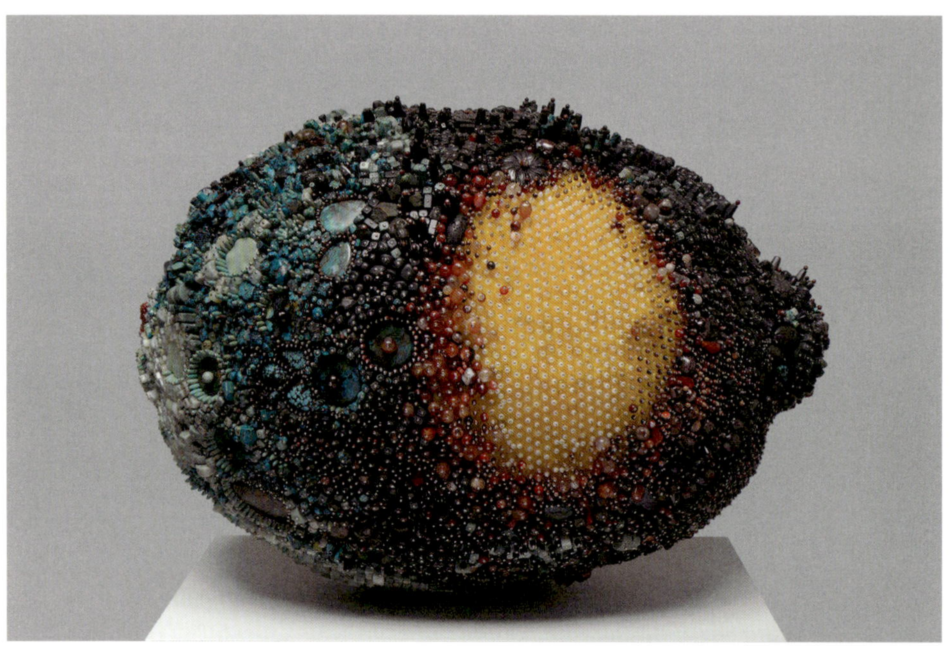

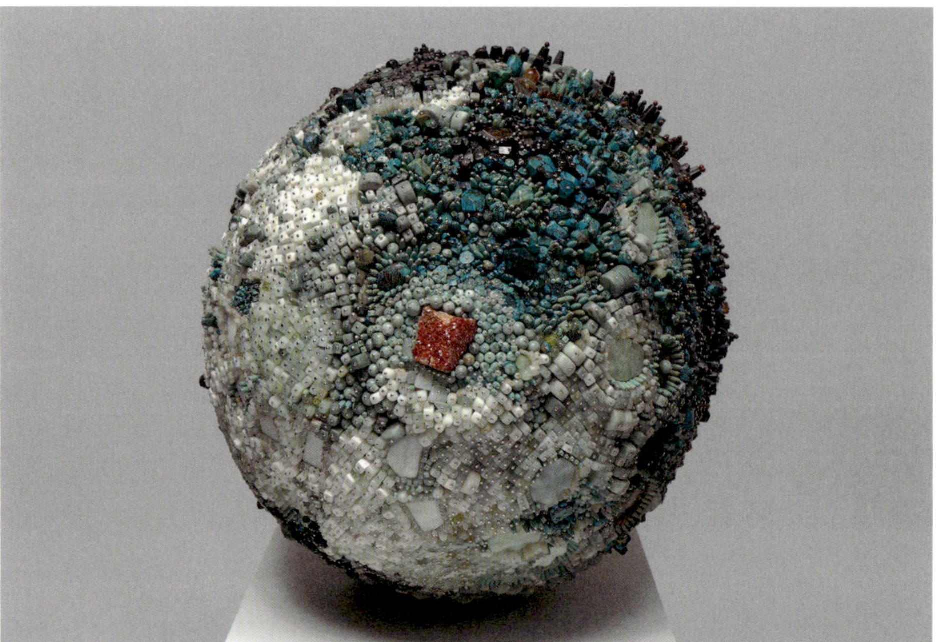

KATHLEEN RYAN, *Bad Lemon (Persephone)*, 2020. Turquoise, serpentine, agate, smoky quartz, labradorite, tiger eye, tektite, zebra jasper, carnelian, garnet, pyrite, black stone, magnesite, Ching Hai jade, aventurine, Italian onyx, mahogany obsidian, vanadinite, glass, and steel pins on coated polystyrene; 19 1/2 x 28 1/2 x 18 inches (49.5 x 72.4 x 45.7 cm). Nasher Museum of Art at Duke University, Durham, North Carolina. Promised gift of Jennifer McCracken New and Jason G. New. © Kathleen Ryan. Courtesy of the artist and Karma, New York.

Kathleen Ryan

BORN IN SANTA MONICA, CALIFORNIA, 1984

I begin by collecting stone and crystal beads, choosing shapes and colors that spark my desire. From them I build my palette. Here, black obsidian fades to the browns of red agate as it closes in on a fresh yellow spot. Elsewhere, turquoise and green serpentine bloom from the black. On bad days, when the earth's demise feels imminent, it brings me pleasure to work with stones and crystals. It feels like an act of reverence to encrust these sculptures with stones—like I'm making a reliquary, but the relics are the stones themselves. These little bits of earth are rare treasures, the sparkling remains of an earlier time. I made this sculpture in the depths of the 2020 pandemic lockdown, and now, in it, I see parallels between the spread of rot and that of the virus: both teeming, replicating, vibrating with life force as their darkness takes over.

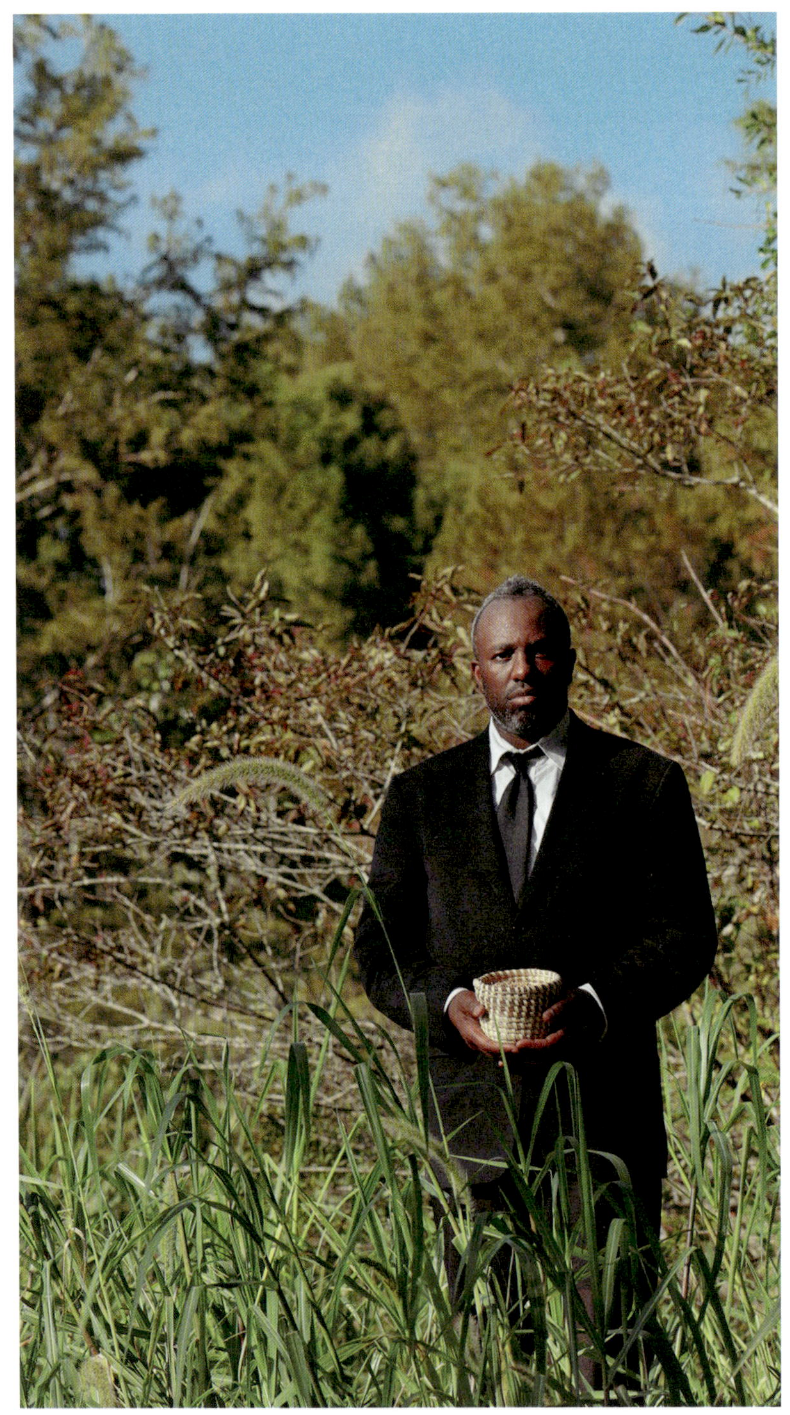

SHELDON SCOTT, Still from *Portrait, number 1 man (day clean ta sun down)*, 2019. Video (color, sound), 12:20 hours. Jon-Sesrie Goff: Cinematography; Tamar-kali: Composition. Courtesy of the artist and CONNERSMITH, Washington, DC. © Sheldon Scott. Photo by Jon-Sesrie Goff.

Sheldon Scott

BORN IN PAWLEYS ISLAND, SOUTH CAROLINA, 1976

saltwater departures

freshwater landings in a crucible birthing a brilliant strength of a brackish people

past, present, and future

you see us, right?

bringing with us old rhythms to new places

in our arms and legs, that we don't cross in your church.

that would be dancing

we sing so loud and stomp so hard because our gods live beyond your heaven

you een see me?

tongues split fo' ways

we lost our form and fell into the shapes of things around us

too much water at the root and we lose our foot

stretch water, take dis 'way from we!

who house dis?

rice welcome the dead

who dead?

eeen me!

who welcome?

eeen we!

youeeen see we?

riz'n in pluff mud

I haffa crak ma teet fo I don get crak

but hunna heay wha I say, but eeen heay wha I mean

youeeen see me yet?

stannin in dis ye wadah

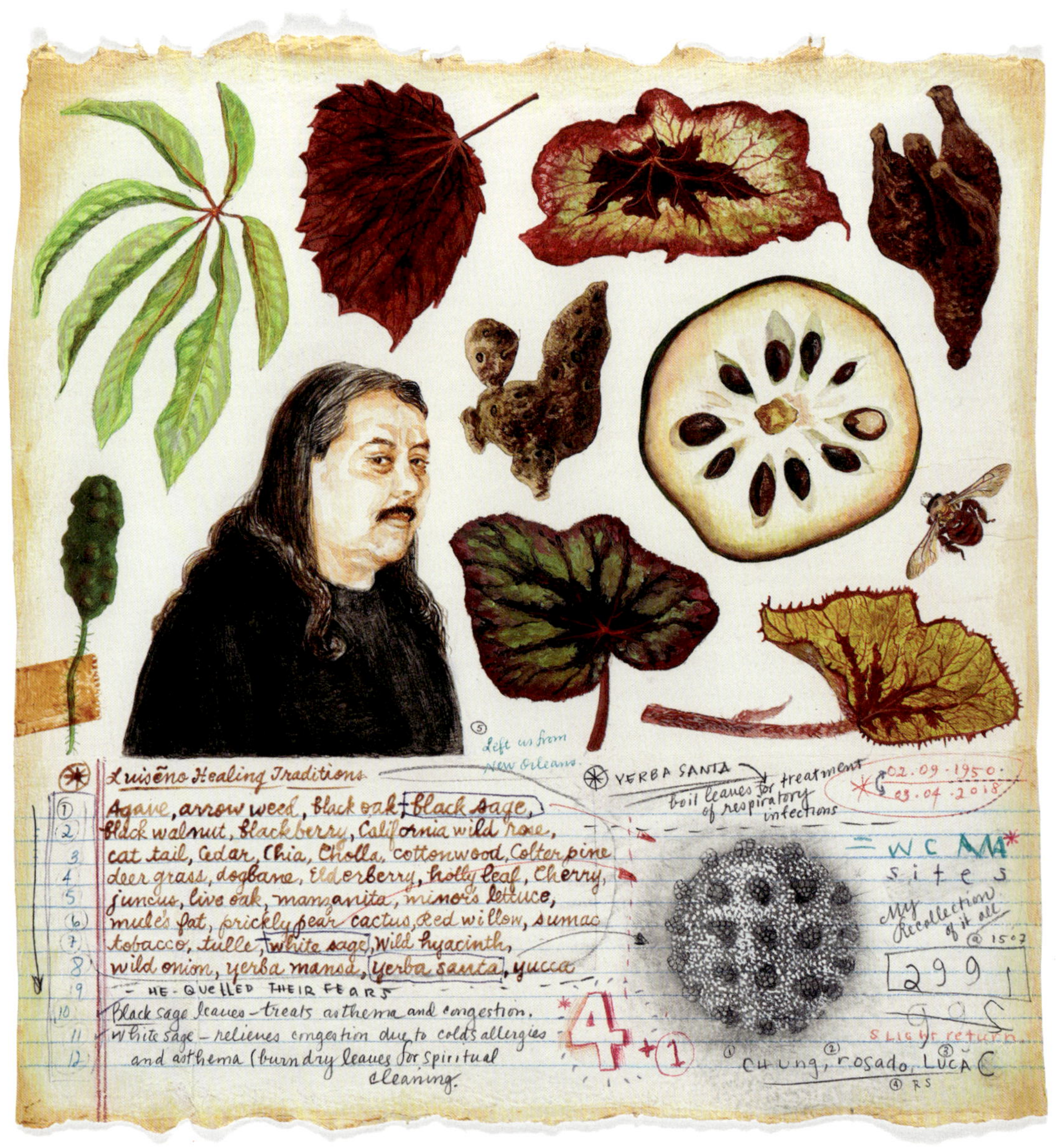

RENÉE STOUT, *Botanical Illustration #3 (The Herbmaster, James Luna)*, 2020. Oil, acrylic, and mixed media on handmade paper; 12 5/16 x 11 13/16 inches (31.3 x 30 cm). Collection of the Nasher Museum of Art at Duke University, Durham, North Carolina. Museum purchase, 2021.23.1. © Renée Stout. Photo by Peter Paul Geoffrion.

Renée Stout

BORN IN JUNCTION CITY, KANSAS, 1958

When I was a little girl, I loved nature so much that whenever someone asked me what I wanted to be when I grew up, my immediate response was "a scientist." At that age, I didn't yet grasp that the field of science has many branches, and that a biologist probably came closest to what I imagined I would be. What I wanted was to be forever connected to the earth and its animals and plants.

I grew up in the East Liberty section of Pittsburgh, Pennsylvania, in a house with a backyard that abutted several acres of dense woods. Within those woods, there was a brook, and many other natural features that sustained all manner of wild creatures like snakes, lizards, and the bats that would circle the yard at dusk.

"The woods" was the place to play for neighborhood kids of all ages. It was a time when parents could let their children go out and play, without worry, because they knew where we were and that we'd eventually make our way back home for dinner. Most summer days, "lunch" was eating berries and other "edibles" from trees and bushes or sucking the "nectar" out of various plants that one of us would tell the other to do on a dare. It's a wonder many of us aren't dead, leading me to believe that this is the true meaning behind the old saying: "God protects fools and babies."

The natural wonders right in my backyard included the two cherry trees that blossomed so beautifully in the spring and stood like sentinels on either side of the swing set at the back end of

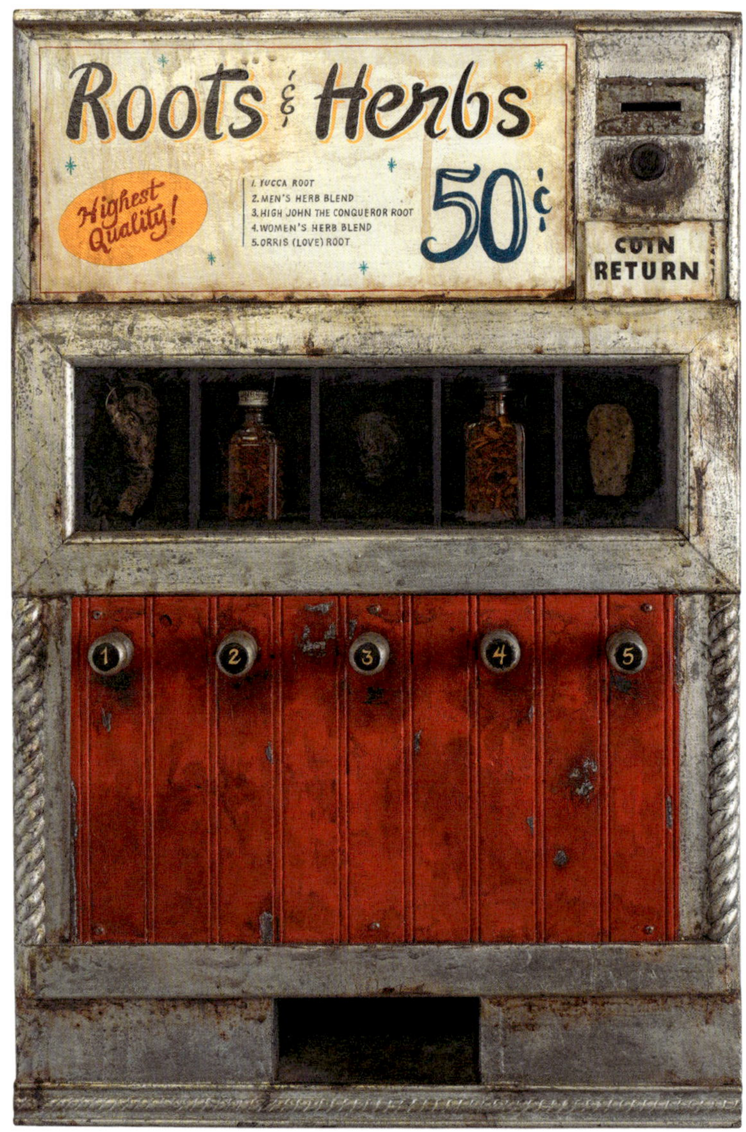

RENÉE STOUT, *Root Dispenser*, 2013. Wood construction, acrylic, silver metal leaf, glass, roots, and bottles containing organic materials; 25 1/2 x 17 x 6 inches (64.8 x 43.2 x 15.2 cm). Collection of the Nasher Museum of Art at Duke University, Durham, North Carolina. Museum purchase with funds provided by Jennifer McCracken New and Jason G. New, 2021.24.1. © Renée Stout. Photo by Brian Quinby.

the yard. One was easy to climb, and I used to love to sit in it and observe the birds, caterpillars, and various insects that moved up and down the shiny mahogany-colored bark on its branches.

A next-door neighbor who had worked at Pittsburgh's Buhl Planetarium observed the hours I spent in the yard examining things and decided that he wanted to encourage my curiosity. He approached my father and asked if he could give me an old microscope that he had stashed away. One evening, my father came in with a wooden box, presented it to me, and said, "This is from Mr. Alexander next door." Opening that box to find a microscope and a little drawer of plain and prepared and labeled slides was one of the highlights of my young life. It took my curiosity about the world around me to a whole new level and enabled me to have a more intimate experience with nature. My parents gave me a chemistry set and a biology set with another microscope the very next Christmas.

My curiosity about the nature in my backyard and its extension, that magical wooded world beyond it, endured into my teenage years. Many times, I spent hours walking through the woods with just my dog, Peppy, as a companion. One of my favorite things to do was to go to the brook and turn rocks and stones over, looking for salamanders. If I found one, I'd hold it in my palm, studying it for a few minutes, then I'd place it back in the water. I loved catching glimpses of snakes winding along the paths.

There was never a time when I didn't collect random seedpods, shells, feathers, bones, insects. Now I've added herbs that are believed to have medicinal and magical qualities. These things find their way into my work as I reinforce my relationship to nature and pay respects to my African Ancestors, who, in their ancient wisdom, worshiped and honored the land that sustained them physically and spiritually.

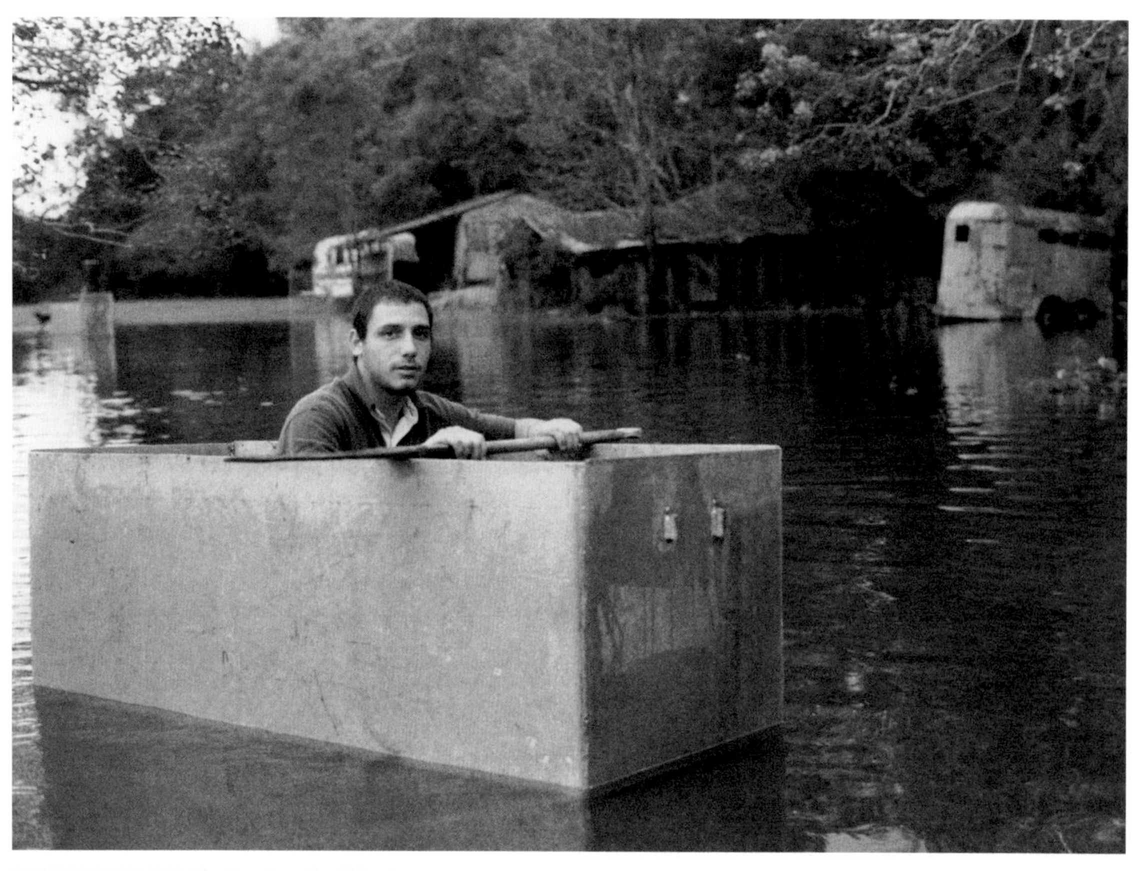

MONIQUE VERDIN, *The New Frontier*, 2004. Inkjet print on paper, 18 x 24 inches (45.7 x 61 cm). Courtesy of the artist. © Monique Verdin.

Monique Verdin

HOUMA NATION, BORN IN BVLBANCHA (NEW ORLEANS),
LOUISIANA, 1980

Our Houma people have been pushed to the edges of in-between territories since the colonizers stepped off the boats and onto the banks of the Mississippi River. Land loss for Indigenous peoples in South Louisiana did not being with climate change; it began centuries earlier as waves of forced migrations, induced by Europeans claiming the high grounds for their plantations, pushed our ancestors to the ends of the bayous where the sacred lands of the Delta, a place that is more water than land, provided a refuge and retreat.

When I was eighteen, my grandmother Armantine Marie Billiot Verdin joined me and elders on a bayou journey down "La Pointe" (The Point), as she would say, to the oak ridge where she was raised, three miles past the Cut-Off Canal in a place called by two names: Pointe-aux-Chênes (Point of the Oaks) and Pointe au-Chien (Point of the Dog), in the heart of the Yakni Chitto (Big Country). What I did not realize that day, as elders reminisced about the oil and gas men coming in to claim our territories as their own, was how we were witnessing the frontlines of climate change and the legacy of side effects caused by corporations.

The Mississippi River is the life force that gives spirit to the land here in South Louisiana, supporting an interface of regeneration and change, producing biological wonders such as cypress forests and oak *chenieres*, flotant marshes, tidal wetlands, and remnants of trembling prairies stretching south to where the sweetwater meets the salty currents of the sea. We are losing land at one of the fastest rates on the planet here in coastal Louisiana. The oversimplified statistic is that every ninety to one hundred minutes a football field is taken back by the rising waters of the Gulf of Mexico, and every year hurricane season sets us in the so-called "cone of uncertainty," as we hunker down for storms of unprecedented frequency and intensity that seem to only increase year to year. Houma communities in the Yakni Chitto and across South Louisiana have been wrestling to adapt, lifting their homes up seventeen to twenty feet, as others contemplate moving further inland to higher grounds. But the truth is, we cannot run from climate change, and there is no place like home.

I have been documenting my relatives and our lifeways at the ends of the bayous since 1998, and it has been a heartbreaking journey to witness and record how quickly the landscape continues to change. There are still a scattering of ancient trees here in our Delta territories that started growing when Columbus embarked on his first voyage across the Atlantic in 1492. I often wonder what those trees would say if they could bear witness to the centuries, and what wisdom they would share for the generations to come.

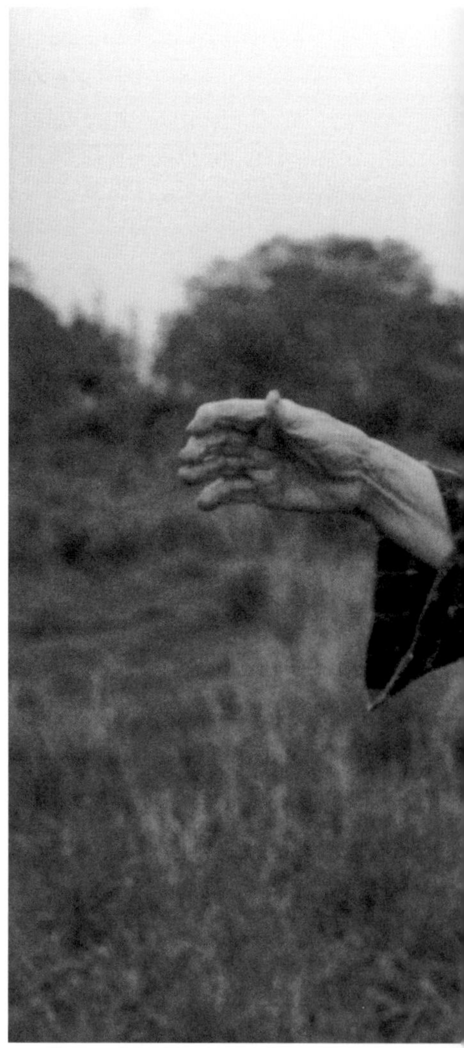

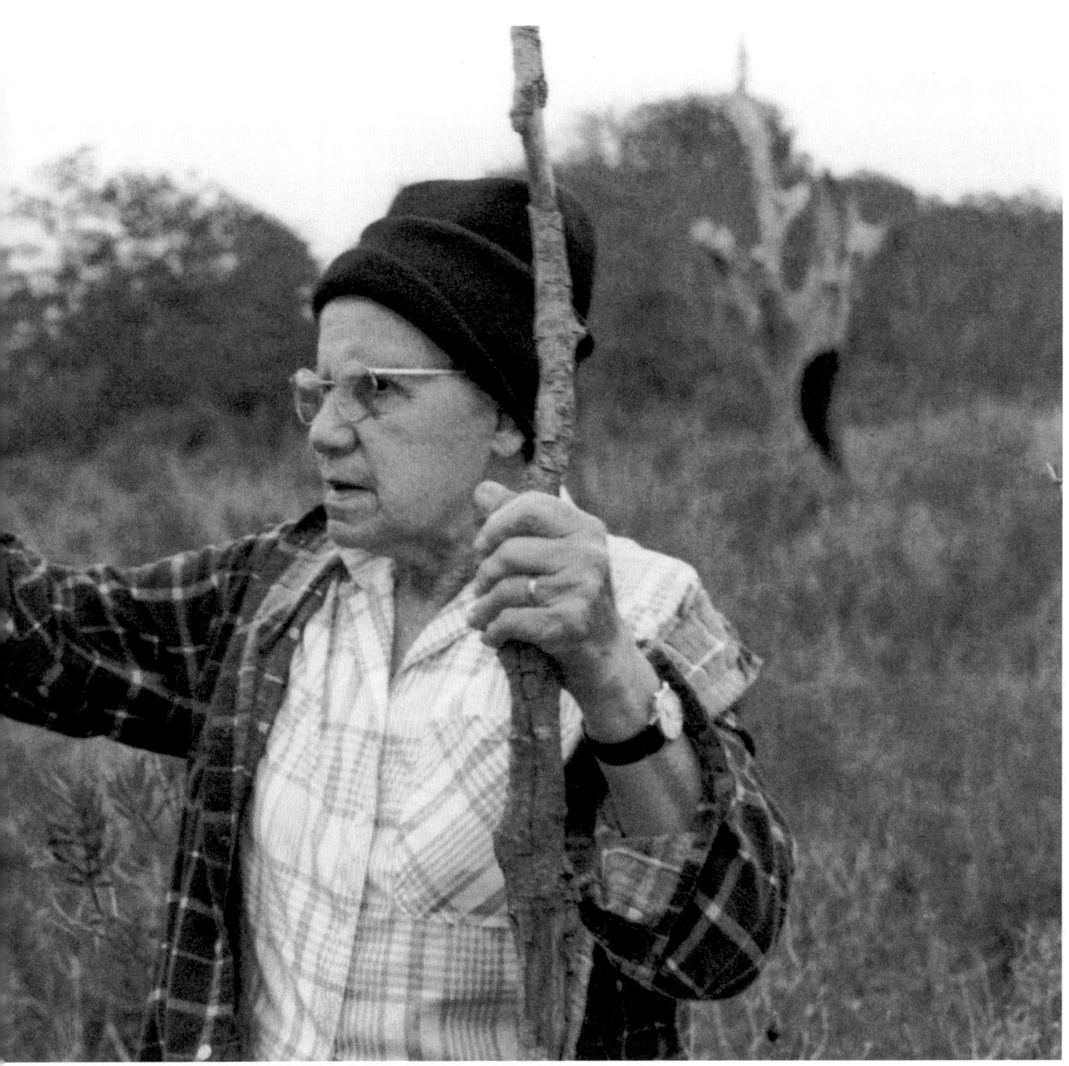

MONIQUE VERDIN, ***Burial Grounds***, 2000. Inkjet print on paper, 12 x 18 inches (30.5 x 45.7 cm). Courtesy of the artist.
© Monique Verdin.

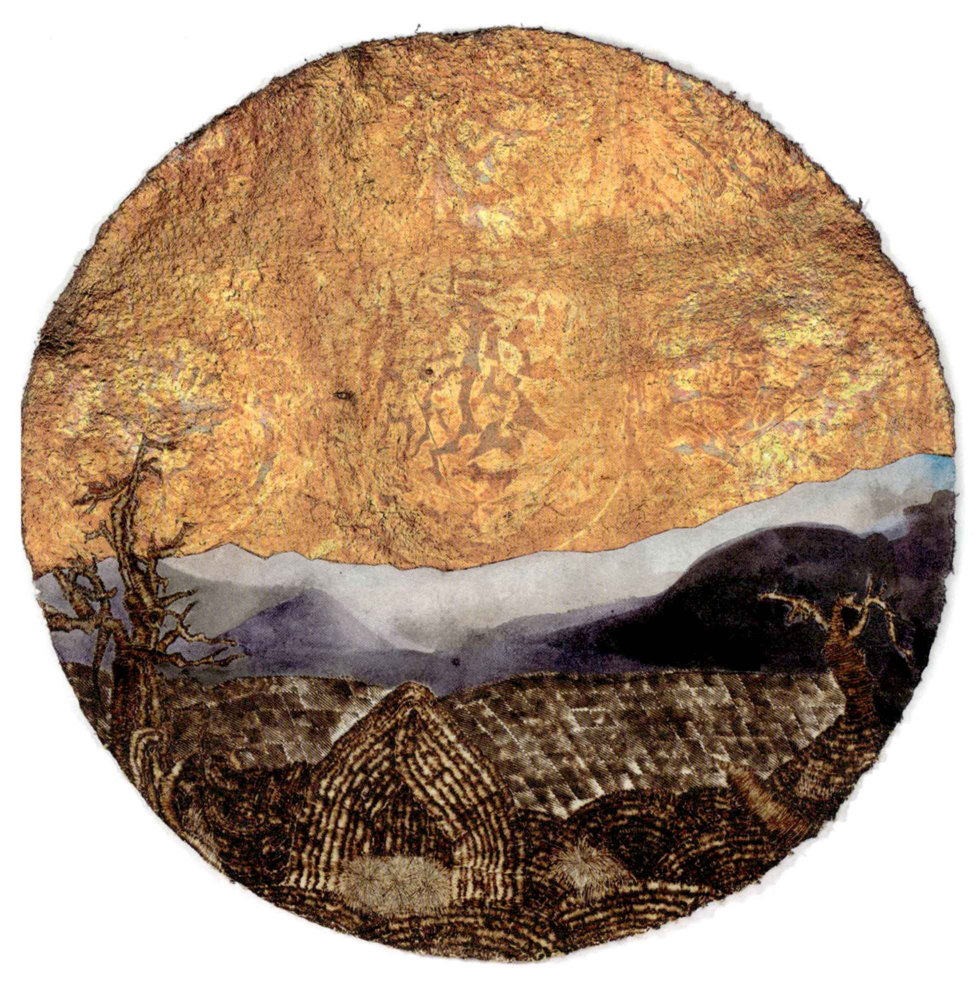

STACY LYNN WADDELL, *A View of Asheville, North Carolina under a Radiant, Infrared Sky (for R.S.D.)*, 1850/2022. Burned handmade paper with blue pencil, ink, and variegated gold leaf; 16 x 16 inches (40.6 x 40.6 cm). Courtesy of the artist and CANDICE MADEY, New York. © Stacy Lynn Waddell. Photo by Brian Quinby.

Stacy Lynn Waddell

BORN IN WASHINGTON, DC, 1966

My relationship to land would begin well before I was born.

In 1947, my great grandfather Zollie Coffey Massenburg built what would become our homehouse on a portion of hilly lands in rural North Carolina. Here, my maternal grandparents would raise a family of seven that has continued to thrive and grow from our beloved farm and pasture lands.

Having never met my great grandfather, I came to know him through stories and anecdotes lovingly shared at gatherings at the homehouse, more commonly referred to as being On The Hill. What stood out most from those reflections was his determined and enterprising spirit. He acquired large tracts of land that he bequeathed to each of his fourteen children in a time and place where Black men and women typically weren't able to initiate enduring security. This legacy ensured that my family's origin story would forever be embedded in the dirt, rocks, trees, and fields that have continued to nurture us.

I grew from a place of buttercups, honeysuckles, and june bugs in a time when children didn't seem to care whether or not they were seen or heard by adults. We preferred the freedom to roam from one experience to the next amongst ourselves. This free range required being out of doors. The woods, fields, and roads we occupied were all too familiar, yet provided an endless array of possibilities. It's a pity that imaginative powers tend to fade as we grow towards adulthood. Space, time, and structures appear but a portion of their former glory, as we naturally give over to rationality and objectivity.

Thankfully, art intervened to ensure those powers would
remain intact.

My landscape works are a means of paying tribute by expanding
historical narratives in order to highlight our ongoing collective
anxieties. Anxieties related to accessibility, ownership, and
our precarious relationship to the natural world haven't much
evolved since the start of the American experiment. In my view,
a nineteenth-century American landscape painting is currently
more instructive than ever as an irreversible global climate
disaster looms large as a result of our failed stewardship of the
natural world.

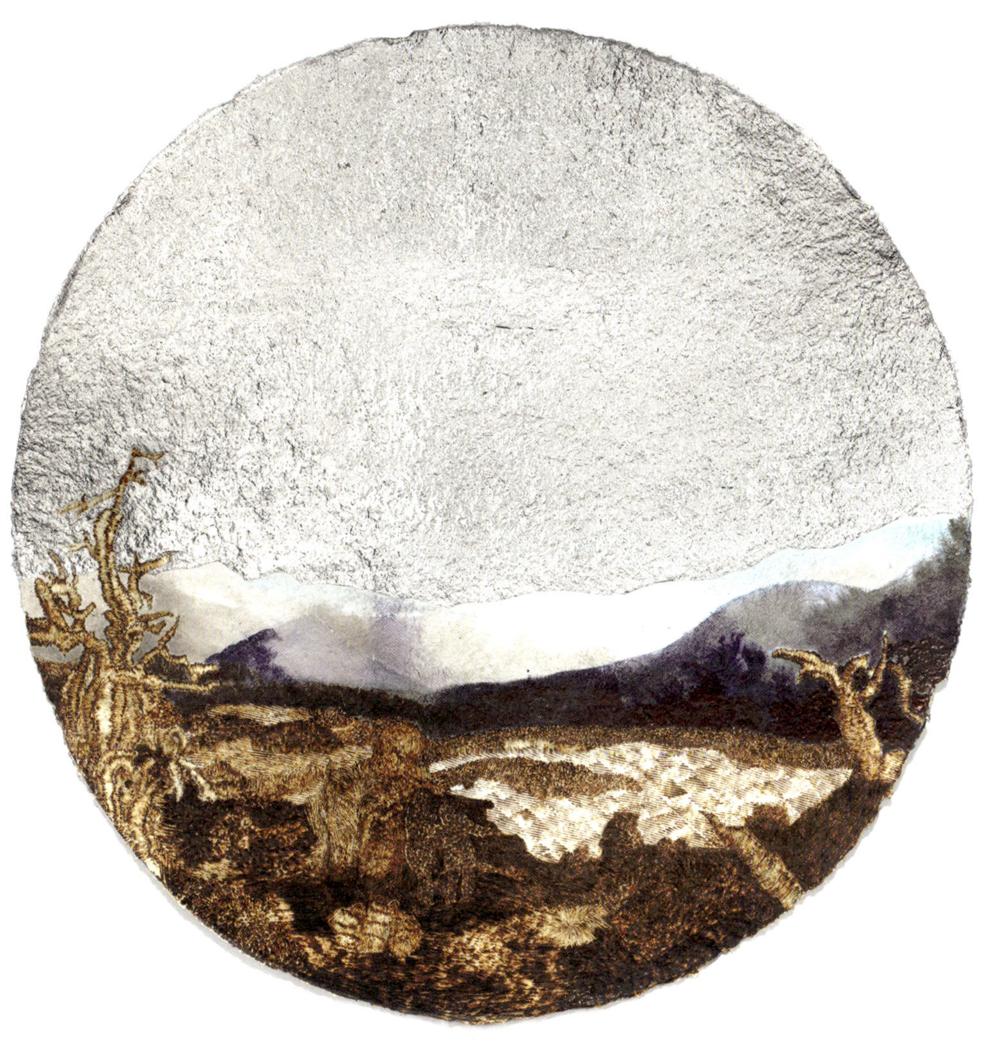

STACY LYNN WADDELL, *A View of Asheville, North Carolina under Dwindling Cloud Cover (for R.S.D.)*,
1850/2022. Burned handmade paper with blue pencil, ink, and aluminum leaf; 16 x 16 inches (40.6 x 40.6 cm).
Courtesy of the artist and CANDICE MADEY, New York. © Stacy Lynn Waddell. Photo by Brian Quinby.

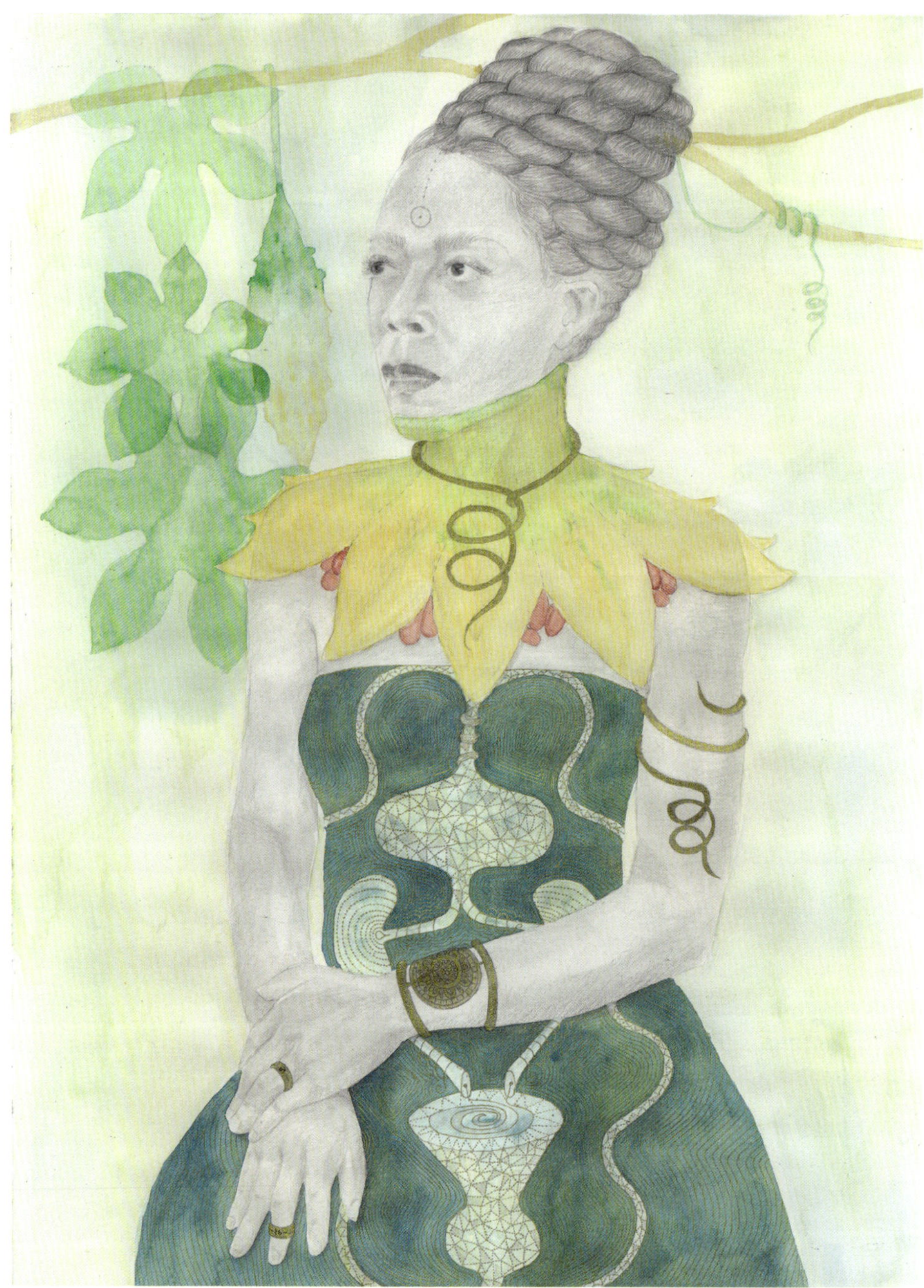

CHARMAINE WATKISS, *The Warriors Way: Restructuring the Self*, 2021. Graphite, pencil, watercolor, and ink on paper; 29 7/8 x 22 1/8 inches (75.9 x 56.2 cm). Collection of the Nasher Museum of Art at Duke University, Durham, North Carolina. Museum purchase, 2022.2.1. © Charmaine Watkiss. Courtesy of the artist and Tiwani Contemporary. Photo by Charmaine Watkiss.

Charmaine Watkiss

BORN IN LONDON, UNITED KINGDOM, 1964

My earliest experiences of having a relationship with the natural world were of my mother treating my brother and myself with herbs. If we had a cough or a fever, my mother would boil herbs into a tea, or rub ointments on our chests to help shift the cold. My mother grew up in St. Thomas in the Blue Mountains, Jamaica. Her family lived off the land, so when she came to live in Great Britain in 1962, she carried the knowledge of her mother and grandmother with her. Like for so many women of her generation, the land and natural healing were important. She passed on some of her knowledge of herbs to me, so I too treat myself naturally whenever I can. I hadn't really thought about exploring the natural world with my drawing practice until fairly recently, and the idea for this evolved from a conversation with a fellow artist who wanted to commission me to undertake drawing research in Elephant and Castle, an area in South East London that historically was working class, and has now been gentrified.

I started to recount stories about how my mother used to send me to a shop called Baldwin's (G Baldwin & Co, established in 1844) to buy herbs. In the 1970s and '80s, a lot of Black women sent their children there to buy sarsaparilla along with herbs and tonics. It occurred to me that I could explore my parent's generation's relationship to herbs and healing. That was my research starting point. Over time, the work developed into a poetic exploration of history, ecology, ancestral knowledge, and themes around colonization. Instead of a linear story, the work evolved into a series of chapters relating to women's strength and courage. Included among these women were a pantheon of fantastical "plant warrior women" created out of the idea that plants, just like

varying stages of spiritual evolution, and when we ingest them
we are taking on the properties of that plant. My warrior women
each have their own planetary ruler and archetype based on plant
mythology and tarot symbolism. *The Warriors Way: Restructuring
the Self* is one such warrior, based on the Cerasee plant; a bitter
gourd when unripe, the extremely bitter leaves were used to make
tea, to act as a purgative. I had purposely chosen to explore
plants that my mother's generation would have used for healing.

Return of the Seed Keeper is specifically connected to the
colonization of plants and humans, but it also connects to the
knowledge that had been transported along with the enslaved.
Within the terrarium is a beautiful flower with a deadly history—
the seeds of the Pride of Barbados, or *Caesalpinia pulcherrima*,
were used as abortifacients and as a poison in acts of liberation
by the enslaved. This work is a record and a memoriam of a
collective past.

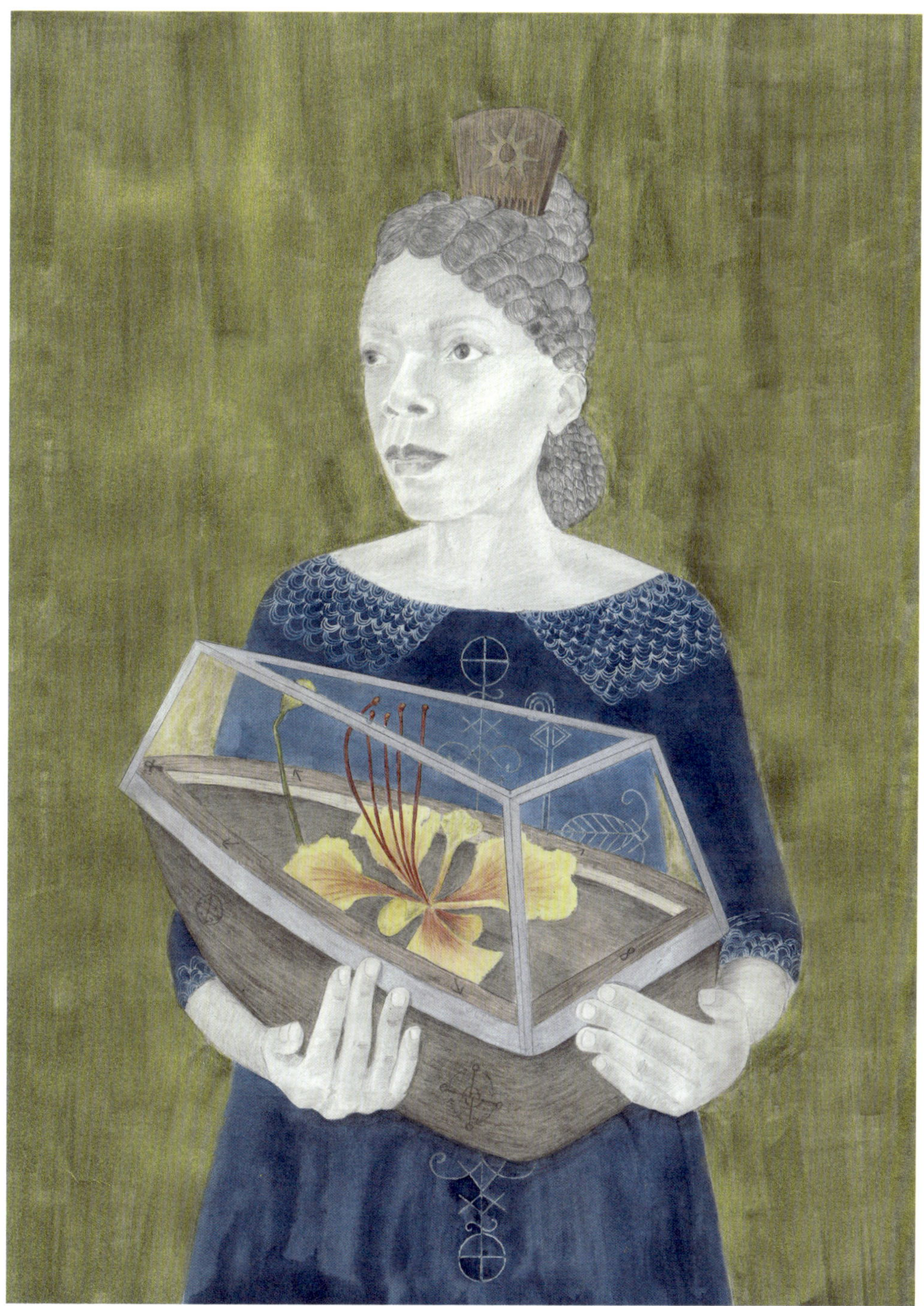

CHARMAINE WATKISS, *Return of the Seed Keeper*, 2021. Graphite, watercolor, ink, and colored pencil on paper; 34 ⁵/₈ x 26 inches (87.9 x 66 cm). Collection of Susan and Michael Hershfield. © Charmaine Watkiss. Courtesy of the artist and Tiwani Contemporary. Photo by Charmaine Watkiss.

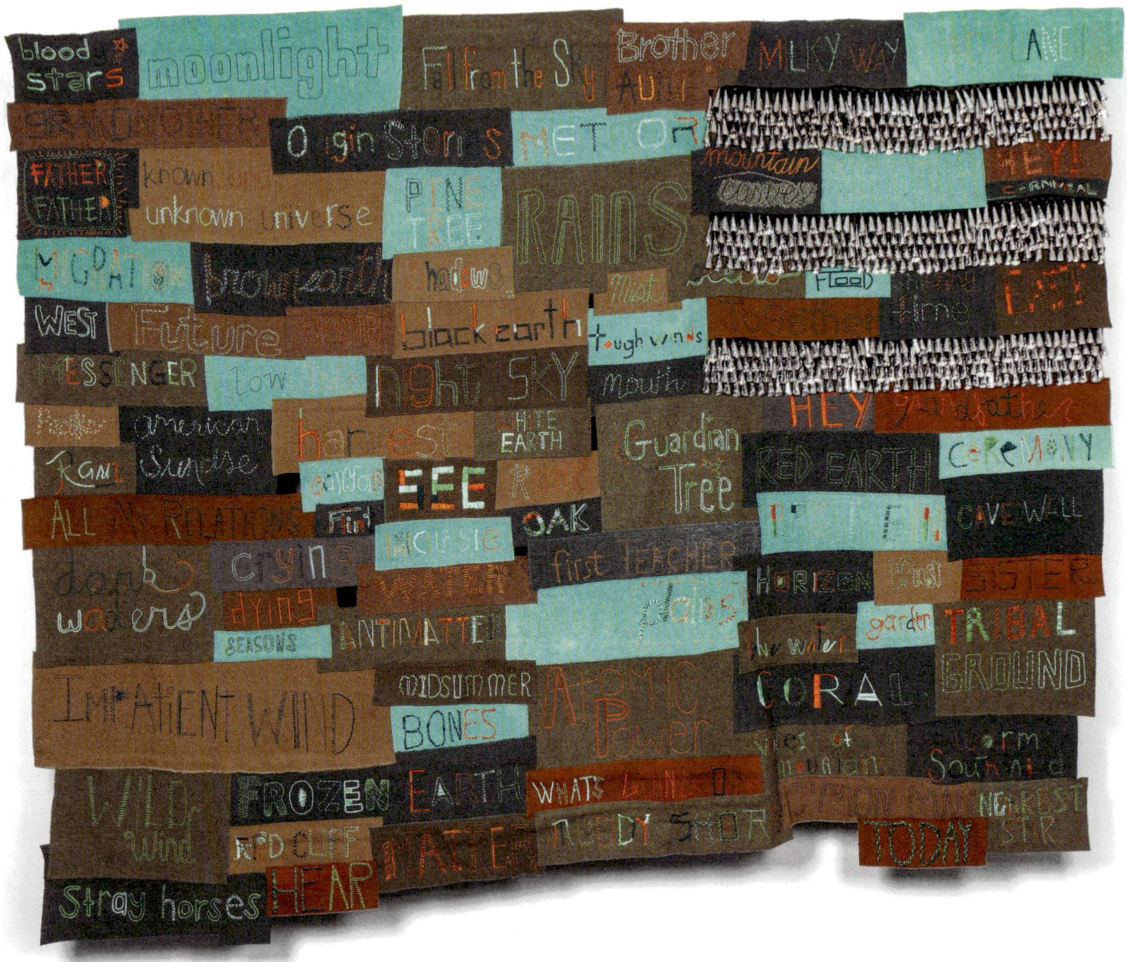

MARIE WATT, *Companion Species: Assembly (Guardian Tree)*, 2020. One panel of the two-part work *Companion Species: Assembly (Auntie and Guardian Tree)*. Reclaimed wool blankets, embroidery floss, thread, cotton twill tape, and tin jingles; 95 x 116 inches (241.3 x 294.6 cm). Tia Collection, Santa Fe, New Mexico. © Marie Watt. Courtesy of MARC STRAUS, New York. Photo by Kevin McConnell. Courtesy of Marie Watt Studio.

Marie Watt

SENECA, BORN IN SEATTLE, WASHINGTON, 1967

What would the world look like if we thought of ourselves as companion species? This is the question that inspired *Companion Species: Assembly (Auntie and Guardian Tree)*. The Seneca believe there is a symbiotic and reciprocal relationship between humans and animals; we believe animals to be our First Teachers. Seeing the world this way foregrounds the connections humans have with nature, and our responsibilities as stewards of the natural world.

Many of the words in this piece come from the poetry of US Poet Laureate Joy Harjo (Muscogee/Creek) and from the Haudenosaunee Thanksgiving Address. (This address is invoked on both regular and special occasions, and is not related to the US holiday.) Some of the words name family relations—*auntie, uncle, grandmother, grandfather*—while others are calls to the natural world—*moonlight, milky way, pine tree, rains*.

The words also reference a song that has always resonated with me—Marvin Gaye's "What's Going On." Throughout the course of this song, Gaye calls out, "Mother mother," "brother brother," "sister sister," "father father," acknowledging his—and our—relatedness. I am interested in the ways that Seneca and Indigenous knowledge about our relatedness intersect with the wisdom in Gaye's song. In Seneca and Indigenous thinking, his call would extend to include "grandmother grandmother, grandfather grandfather, auntie auntie," etc., and would likely continue beyond the human, acknowledging animals and other elements of the natural world as well.

The words are stitched onto wool blankets. I used blankets because these pieces of fabric—whether woven, felted, stitched, or embroidered—have played such a central role in the lives of Indigenous populations in the Americas. Blankets are everyday objects with extraordinary histories. They have served as shelters, shields, armor, flags; they have a long history of use in trade, domestic spaces, war, camping, gifting. Army blankets like the ones in this piece once camouflaged human bodies in the landscape.

The earth has no tongue, but it has its own language. It communicates through natural phenomena like rainfall, hurricanes, sunshine, and drought. As humans, we have tongues to speak for the entities that cannot speak with words. We must remember that we are all part of one ecosystem, and that our bodies are inseparable from the land.

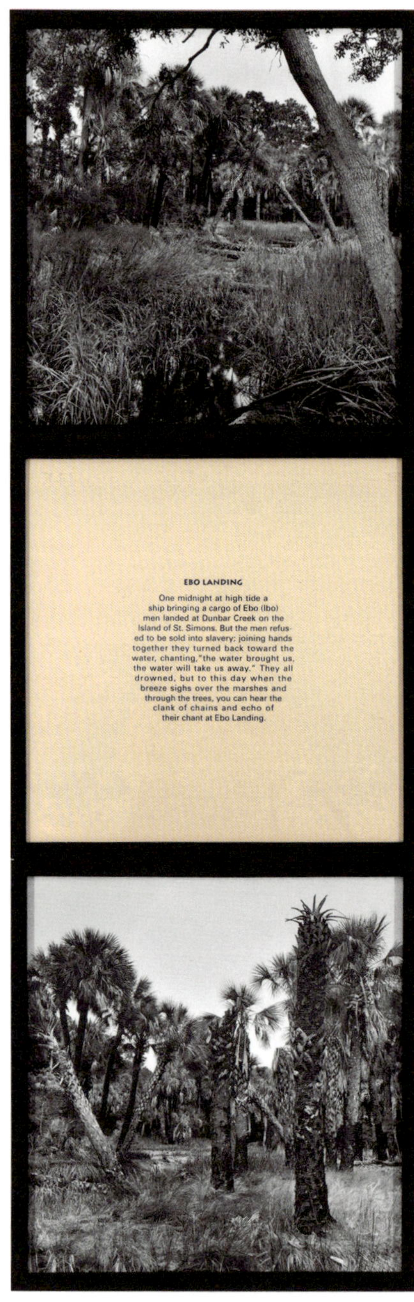

CARRIE MAE WEEMS, *Ebo Landing* from the series *Sea Islands*, 1992. Gelatin silver prints and screenprint on paper, edition 6/10, 60 x 20 inches (152.4 x 50.8 cm) (overall). Collection of the Allen Memorial Art Museum, Oberlin College, Oberlin, Ohio. Gift of Anne and Joel Ehrenkranz, 2016.19.22A-C. © Carrie Mae Weems. Courtesy of the artist and Jack Shainman Gallery, New York.

Carrie Mae Weems

BORN IN PORTLAND, OREGON, 1953

"I am nature imaging the natural world: try as we might,
we cannot separate ourselves from the very thing we are."[1]

— Carrie Mae Weems

One midnight at high tide a
ship bringing a cargo of Ebo (Ibo)
men landed at Dunbar Creek on the
Island of St. Simons. But the men refus-
ed to be sold into slavery; joining hands
together they turned back toward the
water, chanting, "the water brought us,
the water will take us away." They all
drowned, but to this day when the
breeze sighs over the marshes and
through the trees, you can hear the
clank of chains and echo of
their chant at Ebo Landing.[2]

1 Carrie Mae Weems,
email correspondence
with Trevor Schoonmaker,
April 2022.

2 Carrie Mae Weems,
text from *Ebo Landing*
from the series *Sea
Islands*, 1992 (illustrated
adjacent).

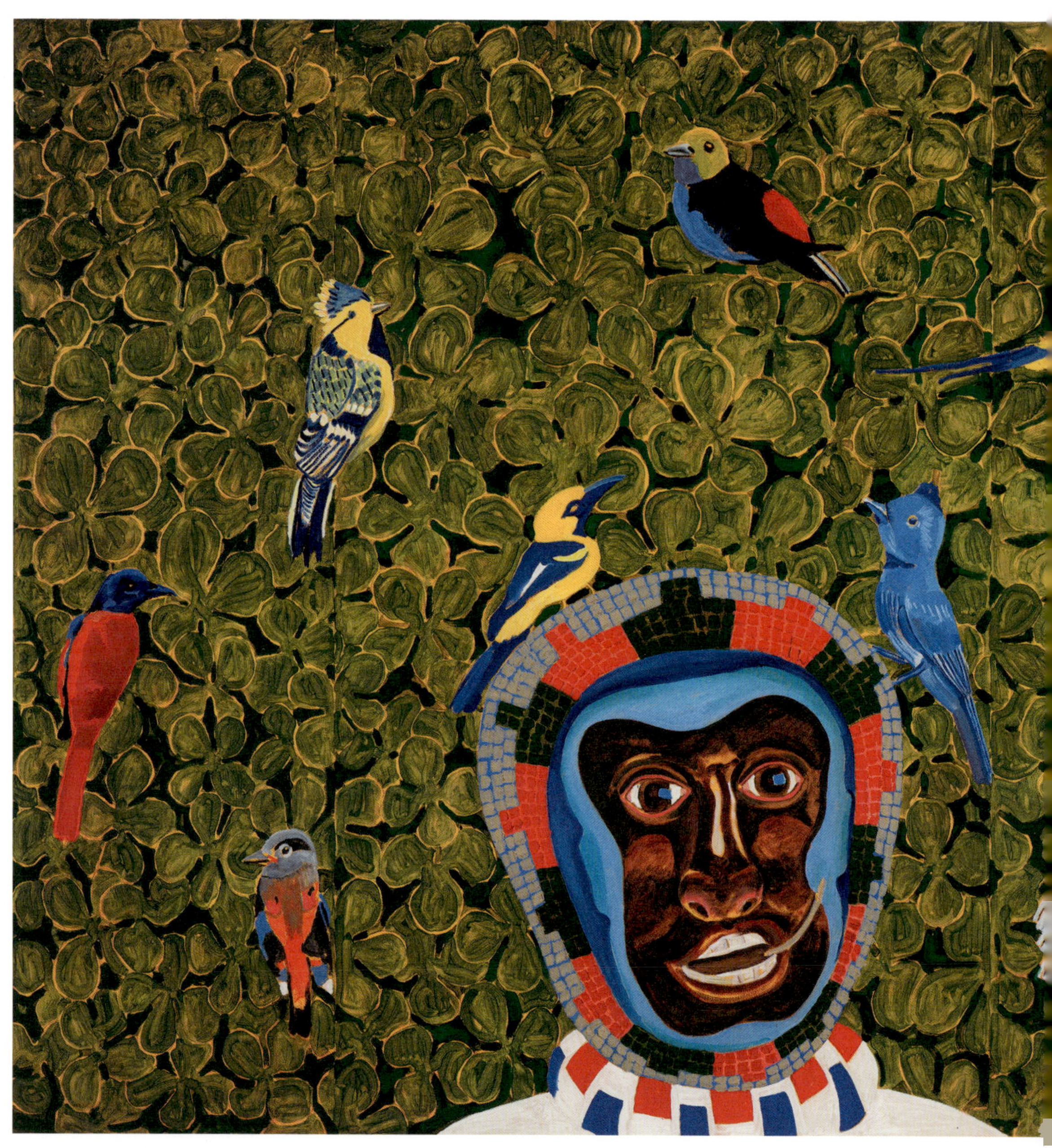

PETER WILLIAMS, *Birdland*, 2020. Oil and graphite on canvas, 60 x 72 inches (152.4 x 182.9 cm). Collection of the Nasher Museum of Art at Duke University, Durham, North Carolina. Museum purchase with funds provided by Stefanie and Douglas Kahn, 2020.17.1. © Estate of Peter Williams. Courtesy of Luis De Jesus Los Angeles. Photo by Peter Paul Geoffrion.

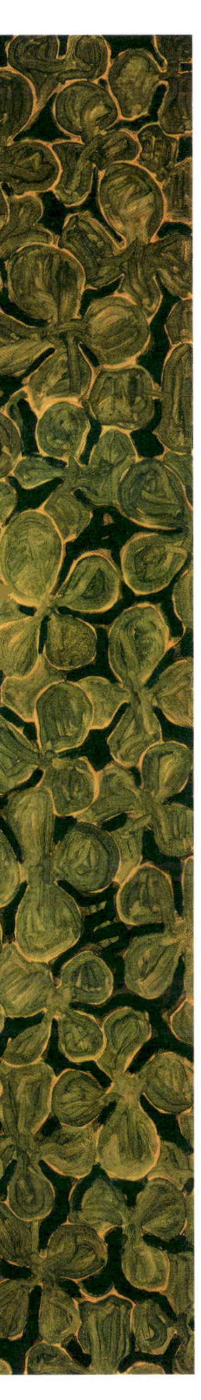

Peter Williams

BORN IN NYACK, NEW YORK, 1952; DIED 2021

"Flights of imagination and themes of transport
have always been at play in my art. These
works envision a journey of consciousness and
conscience, a metaphor for the inner and
outer travels that all of us must undertake to
confront the truth about race and ourselves. The
Black Universe series is anchored in a narrative
of resilience and self-empowerment."[1]

— Peter Williams

Peter's love for nature was an everyday adventure.
He loved to sit outdoors, listen and watch the
birds and wildlife, which have been abundant
here. A red cardinal inside a shrub, the backdrop
of green layers…bright blue jay, titmice, juncos…
his mind registered their beauty, their song. Now
is the time when the old high trees begin to glitter
with thousands of fireflies. He never missed that
show. He had a wooden deck, diamond shaped,
constructed from his painting studio towards
our "forest." There was a plan to build a sculpture
park under these enormous hundred-year-old
beech and oak trees in the back of our house.
Peter marveled at nature's color and form.

The car accident, in which he was a victim as a
barely twenty-year-old art student, altered his life

in many, sometimes unexpected, ways. When I started creating a cottage garden, it needed some landscape adjustments. There was an unexpected problem: Peter hated any trimming back of trees, any cutting of even old and sick branches that needed to go. I discovered that he had projected himself into all trees and shrubs, not only in our backyard. Trees have been present in many of his very stark, dark paintings. I mean those addressing lynchings. They are the silent witnesses of those unspeakably brutal acts. In some, he brings in his versions of "fireflies" to illuminate the darkness of humanity.

We planted nine birch trees to dry out our wet backyard. He became their surrogate, looking out with high concern anytime the skies were too bright, as any father looking at his children mistaking something natural for a catastrophe. His mind was greener than one would imagine.[2]

—Líza Williams

1 Peter Williams, "Statement of Plans," Guggenheim Fellowship application, 2020. Courtesy of Luis De Jesus Los Angeles.

2 Líza Williams, email correspondence with Trevor Schoonmaker, July 2022.

Next page:
CHRISTI BELCOURT, *This Painting Is a Mirror*, 2012.
Acrylic on canvas, 73 x 107 inches (185.4 x 271.8 cm).
Indigenous Art Collection, Crown-Indigenous Relations and Northern Affairs Canada. © Christi Belcourt.
Photo by Lawrence Cook.

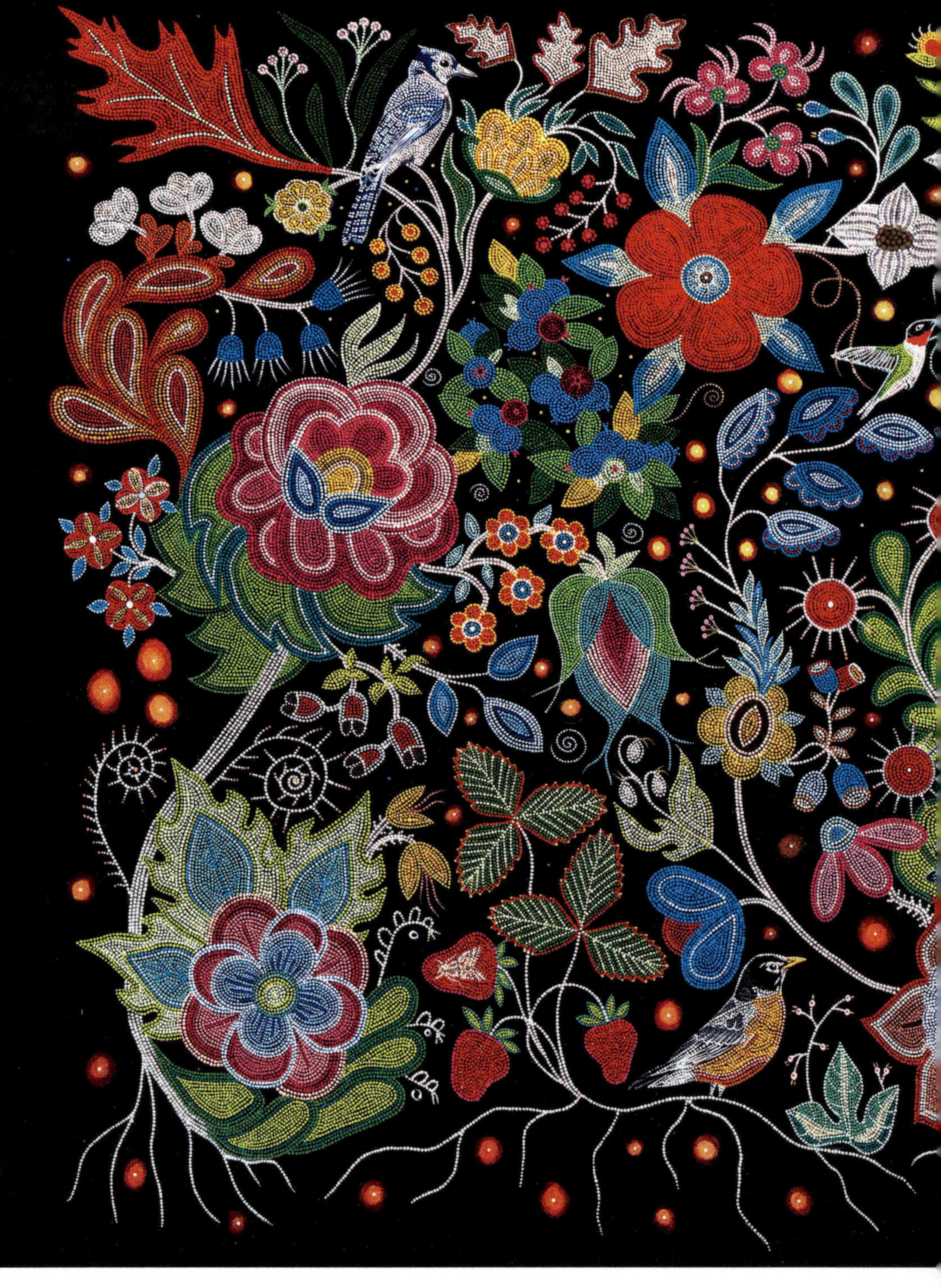

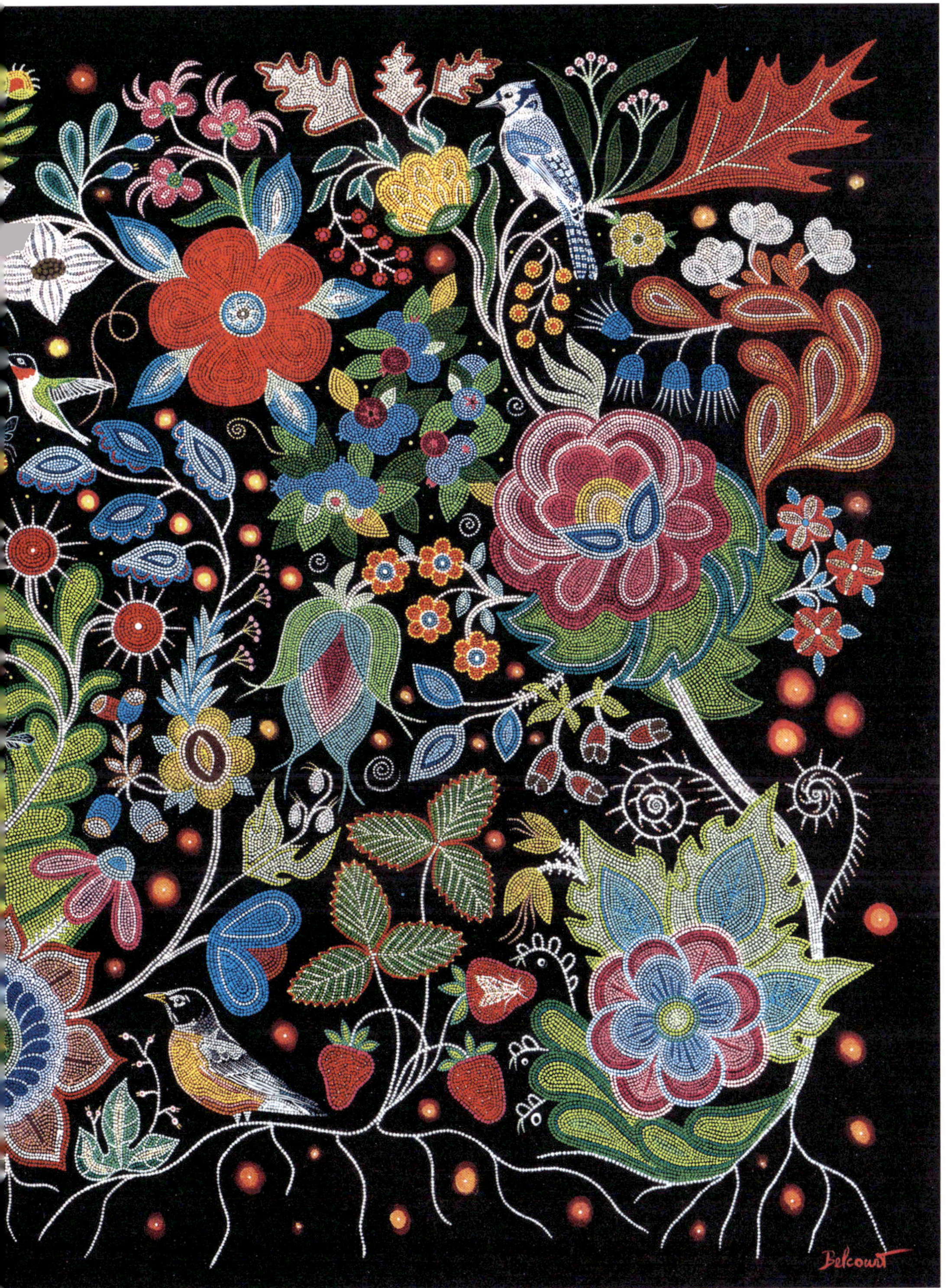
Belcourt

Exhibition Checklist

Terry Adkins

Roost, 2001. Video (color, sound), 9:09 minutes. Courtesy of the artist's
estate and Paula Cooper Gallery, New York.

Firelei Báez

Tignon for Ayda Weddo (or that which a center can not hold), 2019.
Acrylic and oil on archival printed canvas, $91\frac{1}{2}$ x $114\frac{1}{4}$ inches
(232.4 x 290.2 cm). Collection of the Nasher Museum of Art at Duke
University, Durham, North Carolina. Museum purchase, 2019.24.1.

Radcliffe Bailey

King Snake, 2021. Steel, 66 x 11 x $7\frac{1}{2}$ inches (167.6 x 27.9 x 19.1 cm).
The Long Gallery Harlem Collection.

Palm, 2013. Mixed media on paper, 64 x $50\frac{7}{8}$ inches (162.6 x 129.2 cm).
Collection of Susan and Michael Hershfield.

Rina Banerjee

*Summer squash and rice liquor, a fortress of land dropped out of origin,
like five parts too big drifted away to sea.*, 2020. Pearls, paillettes,
plastic, metal beads, fabric, sequins, plastic, thread, and metal;
$65\frac{11}{32}$ x $31\frac{1}{2}$ x $17\frac{23}{32}$ inches (166 x 80 x 45 cm). Courtesy of the artist.

Christi Belcourt

This Painting Is a Mirror, 2012. Acrylic on canvas, 73 x 107 inches (185.4 x
271.8 cm). Indigenous Art Collection, Crown-Indigenous Relations and
Northern Affairs Canada.

María Berrío

Joyas Voladoras, 2021–2022. Collage with Japanese paper on linen,
dimensions variable. Courtesy of the artist and Victoria Miro.

Mel Chin

The Bird is the Word (North Carolina Variation), 2001/2019. *Webster's
Third New International Dictionary*, beeswax, and cherrywood;
11 x 10 x 6 inches (27.9 x 25.4 x 15.2 cm). Lent by The David and Alfred
Smart Museum of Art, The University of Chicago; Purchase, The Paul
and Miriam Kirkley Fund for Acquisitions.

Never Forever: The Cabinets of Conuropsis, 2022. Wood, lacquer,
pigment, steel, handwoven tapestry (dyed cotton), and electronic/
audio components; 60 x 24 x 42 inches (152.4 x 61 x 106.7 cm) (overall).
Courtesy of the artist.

Andrea Chung

Colostrum XX, 2020. Collage, ink, rhinestones, pins, and beads
on paper handmade from traditional birthing cloth; 20 x 17 inches
(50.8 x 43.2 cm). Courtesy of the artist and Tyler Park Presents.

House of the Historians, 2022. Sugarcane bark and leaves, sweetgrass,
excelsior and floral twine; dimensions variable. Courtesy of the artist
and Tyler Park Presents.

Untitled, 2022. Collage, ink, rhinestones, pins, and beads on paper
handmade from traditional birthing cloth; 20 x 17 inches
(50.8 x 43.2 cm). Courtesy of the artist and Tyler Park Presents.

Untitled, 2022. Collage, ink, rhinestones, pins, and beads on paper
handmade from traditional birthing cloth; 20 x 17 inches
(50.8 x 43.2 cm). Courtesy of the artist and Tyler Park Presents.

Untitled, 2022. Collage, ink, rhinestones, pins, and beads on paper
handmade from traditional birthing cloth; 20 x 17 inches
(50.8 x 43.2 cm). Courtesy of the artist and Tyler Park Presents.

VEX XXI, 2020. Collage, ink, rhinestones, pins, and beads on paper
handmade from traditional birthing cloth; 20 x 17 inches
(50.8 x 43.2 cm). Courtesy of the artist and Tyler Park Presents.

VEX XXII, 2020. Collage, ink, rhinestones, pins, and beads on paper
handmade from traditional birthing cloth; 6 x 4 inches (15.2 x 10.2 cm).
Courtesy of the artist and Tyler Park Presents.

Sonya Clark

Heavenly Bound, 2021. Cyanotype on cotton, beads; $8\,^1/_2$ x 22 x 1 inches
(21.6 x 55.9 x 2.5 cm). Courtesy of the artist.

Annalee Davis

From a Garden of Hope, 2021–2022. Ink and latex on paper and
acrylic topographical map hand-painted on wall, 25 x 18 inches
(63.5 x 45.7 cm) (each). Courtesy of the artist.

Tamika Galanis

Catching Shadow, 2021. Video (color, sound), 6:02 minutes. Courtesy of
the artist.

Allison Janae Hamilton

Floridawater II, 2019. Archival pigment print, edition 5/5, 24 x 36 inches
(61 x 91.4 cm). Collection of the Nasher Museum of Art at Duke
University, Durham, North Carolina. Museum purchase with funds
provided by The Durham (NC) Chapter of The Links, Incorporated;
2021.13.1.

Sisters, Wakulla County FL, 2019. Archival pigment print, edition 2/5,
24 x 36 inches (61 x 91.4 cm). Collection of the Nasher Museum of
Art at Duke University, Durham, North Carolina. Museum purchase
with funds provided by The Durham (NC) Chapter of The Links,
Incorporated; 2021.13.2.

When the wind has teeth. from the series *Sweet milk in the badlands.*,
2015. Archival pigment print, edition 1/5, 40 x 60 inches (101.6 x
152.4 cm). Collection of the Nasher Museum of Art at Duke University,
Durham, North Carolina. Museum purchase with funds provided
by The Durham (NC) Chapter of The Links, Incorporated; 2021.13.3.

Barkley L. Hendricks

Cocoa Pod from My Man Sammy, 1996. Oil and gold leaf on linen canvas,
$12^7/_8$ x $10^7/_8$ inches (32.7 x 27.6 cm). Courtesy of The Estate of
Barkley L. Hendricks and Jack Shainman Gallery, New York.

Happy Birthday (For Martin), 1982. Oil and aluminum leaf on linen canvas,
$13^1/_2$ x $13^1/_2$ inches (34.3 x 34.3 cm). Courtesy of The Estate of Barkley
L. Hendricks and Jack Shainman Gallery, New York.

Judy's Uneaten Fruit, 1996. Oil and gold leaf on linen canvas, $7^1/_2$ inches
(19.1 cm) (diameter). Courtesy of The Estate of Barkley L. Hendricks
and Jack Shainman Gallery, New York.

Naseberries, 2010. Oil and gold leaf on linen canvas, $11^1/_8$ inches
(28.3 cm) (diameter). Courtesy of The Estate of Barkley L. Hendricks
and Jack Shainman Gallery, New York.

Sweet Sop Sue, 2009. Oil and gold leaf on linen canvas, $11^1/_4$ inches
(28.6 cm) (diameter). Courtesy of The Estate of Barkley L. Hendricks
and Jack Shainman Gallery, New York.

Treasure Birds (Thoughts of Christmas), 1999. Oil on canvas, $21^1/_2$ inches
(54.6 cm) (diameter). Collection of the Nasher Museum of Art at
Duke University, Durham, North Carolina. Gift of Susan and Barkley
L. Hendricks to commemorate naming Trevor Schoonmaker as Mary
D.B.T. and James H. Semans Director of the Nasher Museum of Art
at Duke University, 2020.6.1.

Under Zim's Tree, 1998. Oil on canvas, 17$\frac{1}{4}$ inches (43.8 cm) (diameter). Collection of the Nasher Museum of Art at Duke University, Durham, North Carolina. Gift of Susan and Barkley L. Hendricks to commemorate naming Trevor Schoonmaker as Mary D.B.T. and James H. Semans Director of the Nasher Museum of Art at Duke University, 2020.6.2.

Alexa Kleinbard

Arnica from the series *REMEDIES*, 2003–2008. Oil on birchwood, 45$\frac{1}{2}$ x 36 inches (115.6 x 91.4 cm). Collection of Frank and Peper Willis.

Mayapple and Senna from the series *REMEDIES*, 2003–2008. Oil on birchwood, 44$\frac{1}{2}$ x 33 inches (113 x 83.8 cm). Courtesy of the artist.

Passion Flower from the series *REMEDIES*, 2003–2008. Oil on birchwood, 44$\frac{1}{2}$ x 33 inches (113 x 83.8 cm). Courtesy of the artist.

Hung Liu

Dandelion with Red Dragonfly (silver), 2020. Mixed media, 48 x 48 inches (121.9 x 121.9 cm). Collection of the Nasher Museum of Art at Duke University, Durham, North Carolina. Museum purchase, 2021.21.1.

Hew Locke

Mosquito Hall, 2013. Acrylic on chromogenic print, 83$\frac{7}{8}$ x 49$\frac{3}{4}$ inches (213 x 126.4 cm). Collection of the Nasher Museum of Art at Duke University, Durham, North Carolina. Museum purchase, 2022.22.1.

Tranquility Hall, 2013. Acrylic on chromogenic print, 83$\frac{7}{8}$ x 49$\frac{3}{4}$ inches (213 x 126.4 cm). Courtesy of the artist, Hales Gallery, and P•P•O•W.

Meryl McMaster

From a Still Unquiet Place from the series *As Immense as the Sky*, 2019. Chromogenic print mounted on aluminum composite panel, 40 x 60 inches (101.6 x 152.4 cm). Courtesy of the artist and Stephen Bulger Gallery and Pierre-François Ouellette art contemporain.

My Destiny is Entwined With Yours from the series *As Immense as the Sky*, 2019. Chromogenic print mounted on aluminum composite panel, 40 x 60 inches (101.6 x 152.4 cm). Courtesy of the artist and Stephen Bulger Gallery and Pierre-François Ouellette art contemporain.

Wangechi Mutu

Flying Root IV, 2017. Red soil, paper pulp, wood glue, wood, and cow horns; 23 x 16 x 17 inches (58.4 x 40.6 x 43.2 cm). Courtesy of the artist and Gladstone Gallery.

MamaRay, 2020. Bronze, edition 1/3, 65 x 144 x 192 inches (165.1 x 365.8 x 487.7 cm). Commissioned by and collection of the Nasher Museum of Art at Duke University, Durham, North Carolina. Gift of Mike and Joan Kahn in honor of Douglas and Stefanie Kahn, 2020.18.1.

Subterranea Flourish, 2021. Ink and emulsion paint on photographic print, 72 x 48 inches (182.9 x 121.9 cm). Private collection, California.

Maia Cruz Palileo

Conference of the Birds, 2019. Oil on linen, 60 x 52 inches (152.4 x 132.1 cm). Private collection, courtesy Monique Meloche Gallery.

The Way Back, 2018. Oil on canvas, $59\frac{1}{2}$ x $47\frac{1}{2}$ inches (151.1 x 120.7 cm). Collection of the Nasher Museum of Art at Duke University, Durham, North Carolina. Gift of Jennifer McCracken New and Jason G. New, 2019.6.1.

Dario Robleto

The Naturalist's Lament, 2017. Cut paper, various cut and polished seashells, urchin spines, green tusks, squilla claws, mushroom coral, colored powder pigments and beads, colored crushed glass and wire, plastic domes, prints on paper, colored and mirrored Plexiglas, foam core, glue, and frame; $51\frac{7}{16}$ x $39\frac{1}{4}$ x $3\frac{1}{2}$ inches (130.7 x 99.7 x 8.9 cm). Courtesy of the artist.

Jim Roche

Return to Florida, All in My Background: Piece, 1973–1974. Installation of eight pairs of gelatin silver prints and graphite works on paper, 20 x 16 inches (50.8 x 40.6 cm) (each panel). Collection of the Nasher Museum of Art at Duke University, Durham, North Carolina. Museum purchase and partial gift of Ken Rollins, President, Rollins Fine Art; 2016.19.1.

Kathleen Ryan

Bad Lemon (Persephone), 2020. Turquoise, serpentine, agate, smoky quartz, labradorite, tiger eye, tektite, zebra jasper, carnelian, garnet, pyrite, black stone, magnesite, Ching Hai jade, aventurine, Italian onyx, mahogany obsidian, vanadinite, glass, and steel pins on coated polystyrene; $19\,{}^{1}/_{2}$ x $28\,{}^{1}/_{2}$ x 18 inches (49.5 x 72.4 x 45.7 cm). Nasher Museum of Art at Duke University, Durham, North Carolina. Promised gift of Jennifer McCracken New and Jason G. New.

Sheldon Scott

Portrait, number 1 man (day clean ta sun down), 2019. Video (color, sound), 12:20 hours. Jon-Sesrie Goff: Cinematography; Tamar-kali: Composition. Courtesy of the artist and CONNERSMITH, Washington, DC.

Renée Stout

Botanical Illustration #3 (The Herbmaster, James Luna), 2020. Oil, acrylic, and mixed media on handmade paper; $12\,{}^{5}/_{16}$ x $11\,{}^{13}/_{16}$ inches (31.3 x 30 cm). Collection of the Nasher Museum of Art at Duke University, Durham, North Carolina. Museum purchase, 2021.23.1.

High John the Conqueroo is in My Blood, 2022. Acrylic, ballpoint pen, and graphite on handmade paper; 12 x $11\,{}^{1}/_{2}$ inches (30.5 x 29.2 cm). Courtesy of the artist and MARC STRAUS, New York.

Root Dispenser, 2013. Wood construction, acrylic, silver metal leaf, glass, roots, and bottles containing organic materials; $25\,{}^{1}/_{2}$ x 17 x 6 inches (64.8 x 43.2 x 15.2 cm). Collection of the Nasher Museum of Art at Duke University, Durham, North Carolina. Museum purchase with funds provided by Jennifer McCracken New and Jason G. New, 2021.24.1.

Monique Verdin

Abandoned Camp on Vanishing Land, 2000. Inkjet print on paper, 12 x 18 inches (30.5 x 45.7 cm). Courtesy of the artist.

After the Storm, 2008. Inkjet print on paper, 18 x 12 inches (30.5 x 45.7 cm). Courtesy of the artist.

Anesie Verdin at Home, 2008. Inkjet print on paper, 12 x 18 inches (30.5 x 45.7 cm). Courtesy of the artist.

Bayou Boat Ride, 2008. Inkjet print on paper, 18 x 24 inches (45.7 x 61 cm). Courtesy of the artist.

Burial Grounds, 2000. Inkjet print on paper, 12 x 18 inches (30.5 x 45.7 cm). Courtesy of the artist.

Kid's Truck, 2000. Inkjet print on paper, 12 x 18 inches (30.5 x 45.7 cm). Courtesy of the artist.

Louisiana Lost Treasure Map: Isle de Jean Charles, 2017. Inkjet print on metal, 18 x 24 inches (45.7 x 61 cm). Courtesy of the artist.

Louisiana Lost Treasure Map: Pointe Barre: Vivian Molinere Hotard, 2017. Inkjet print on metal, 18 x 24 inches (45.7 x 61 cm). Courtesy of the artist.

The New Frontier, 2004. Inkjet print on paper, 18 x 24 inches (45.7 x 61 cm). Courtesy of the artist.

Tree of Life, 2000. Inkjet print on paper, 18 x 12 inches (45.7 x 30.5 cm). Courtesy of the artist.

Veronica's Net, 2000. Inkjet print on paper, 12 x 18 inches (30.5 x 45.7 cm). Courtesy of the artist.

Stacy Lynn Waddell

A View of Asheville, North Carolina under a Radiant, Infrared Sky (for R.S.D.), 1850/2022. Burned handmade paper with blue pencil, ink, and variegated gold leaf; 16 x 16 inches (40.6 x 40.6 cm). Courtesy of the artist and CANDICE MADEY, New York.

A View of Asheville, North Carolina under an Atmospheric River Sky (for R.S.D.), 1850/2022. Burned handmade paper with blue pencil, ink, and colored silver leaf; 16 x 16 inches (40.6 x 40.6 cm). Courtesy of the artist and CANDICE MADEY, New York.

A View of Asheville, North Carolina under Dwindling Cloud Cover (for R.S.D.), 1850/2022. Burned handmade paper with blue pencil, ink, and aluminum leaf; 16 x 16 inches (40.6 x 40.6 cm). Courtesy of the artist and CANDICE MADEY, New York.

Charmaine Watkiss

Return of the Seed Keeper, 2021. Graphite, watercolor, ink, and colored pencil on paper; $34\,^5/_8$ x 26 inches (87.9 x 66 cm). Collection of Susan and Michael Hershfield.

The Warriors Way: Restructuring the Self, 2021. Graphite, pencil, watercolor, and ink on paper; $29\,^7/_8$ x $22\,^1/_8$ inches (75.9 x 56.2 cm). Collection of the Nasher Museum of Art at Duke University, Durham, North Carolina. Museum purchase, 2022.2.1.

Marie Watt

Companion Species: Assembly (Guardian Tree), 2020. Reclaimed wool
blankets, embroidery floss, thread, cotton twill tape, and tin jingles;
95 x 116 inches (241.3 x 294.6 cm). Tia Collection, Santa Fe, New Mexico.

Carrie Mae Weems

Box Spring in Tree from the series *Sea Islands*, 1992. Gelatin silver print,
artist's proof 1, 20 x 20 inches (50.8 x 50.8 cm). Courtesy of the artist
and Jack Shainman Gallery, New York.

Ebo Landing from the series *Sea Islands*, 1992. Gelatin silver prints and
screenprint on paper, edition 6/10, 60 x 20 inches (152.4 x 50.8 cm)
(overall). Collection of the Allen Memorial Art Museum, Oberlin College,
Oberlin, Ohio. Gift of Anne and Joel Ehrenkranz, 2016.19.22A-C.

Peter Williams

Birdland, 2020. Oil and graphite on canvas, 60 x 72 inches (152.4 x 182.9
cm). Collection of the Nasher Museum of Art at Duke University,
Durham, North Carolina. Museum purchase with funds provided by
Stefanie and Douglas Kahn, 2020.17.1.

Lenders to the Exhibition

*Thank you to the artists who lent their work to the exhibition,
in addition to:*

Estate of Terry Adkins

Allen Memorial Art Museum

Stephen Bulger Gallery

CONNERSMITH.

Paula Cooper Gallery

Gladstone Gallery

Hales Gallery

Estate of Barkley L. Hendricks

Susan and Michael Hershfield

Indigenous Art Collection,
  Crown-Indigenous Relations
  and Northern Affairs Canada

The Long Gallery Harlem
  Collection

CANDICE MADEY

Monique Meloche Gallery

Victoria Miro

Nasher Museum of Art at Duke
  University

Jennifer McCracken New and
  Jason G. New

Pierre-François Ouellette
  art contemporain

P•P•O•W

Tyler Park Presents

Private collections

Jack Shainman Gallery

Smart Museum of Art,
  The University of Chicago

MARC STRAUS

Tia Collection

Frank and Peper Willis

Nasher Museum of Art at Duke University

Staff

D'Nidra Allen

Yunkee Alston

David Burroughs

Ruth Caccavale

J Caldwell

Jon Carpenter

Alan Dippy

Claire Dubnansky

Deirdre Ellis

Melissa Gwynn

Mindy Hale

Thomas Hamilton

Bryan Hilley

Wendy Hower

Brad Johnson

Joel Johnson

Travis Johnson

Rob Knebel

Amanda Koelling

Patrick Krivacka

Joseph Lallier

Tracey Lannon

Emilie Luse

Julia McHugh

Julianne Miao

Sean Mohlmann

Lee Nisbet

Liz Peters

Marshall Price

Ellen Raimond

Trevor Schoonmaker

Edwin Smith

Sydney Steen

Gabrielle Tenedero

Jay Vestal

Doug Vuncannon

Carolyn Watson

Stephanie Wheatley

Kelly Woolbright

Aaron Zalonis

Amanda Zarate

Board of Advisors

Nancy A. Nasher,
Chair

Less Arnold

Dr. Andrea Barnwell
Brownlee

Christopher M. Bass

Trent A. Carmichael

Maximilian F.
Feidelson

David J. Haemisegger

Jolie J. Johnson

Stefanie S. Kahn

Katherine T. Kerr

Gerrity Lansing, Jr.

Patricia R. Morton

Jennifer McCracken
New

Odili Donald Odita

Katharine L. Reid*

Dario Robleto

Jason L. Rubell

Heather J. Sargent

Douglas Smooke

Tanya Traykovski

Marie B. Washington

Christine H. Weller

Derek M. Wilson

Ex Officio

John Brown

Paul B. Jaskot

Sally Kornbluth

Richard J. Powell

Trevor Schoonmaker

Collections Committee

Thomas S. Rankin,
Chair

Jasmine Nichole
Cobb

Frank Konhaus

Kristine Stiles

Friends Board

Karen Rabenau,
President

Michelle Hooper,
President Elect

Mavis Gragg,
Vice President

Jennings Brody,
Ex Officio

David Arthur

Michelle Beischer

Danny Bell

Ellen Cassilly

Ann Craver

*Deceased

Carter Cue

David Ebershoff

Danielle Gray

Elaine Hart-Brothers

Bryan Huffman

Stacey Kirby

Marjorie Brown
Pierson

Doren Madey Pinnell

Annette Newmeyer
Price

Daniel Robinson

Arthur Rogers

Sanyin Siang

Mindy Solie

Damian Stamer

Lori Arthur Stroud

Marcy Tucker

Stacy Lynn Waddell

Tim Warmath

**Faculty Advisory
Committee**

John Brown
*Vice Provost
for the Arts and
Professor of the
Practice of Music*

Sheila Dillon
*Anne Murnick
Cogan
Distinguished
Professor of Art &
Art History*

Laurent Dubois
*John L. Nau III
Bicentennial
Professor in the
History & Principles
of Democracy,
University of
Virginia*

Esther Gabara
*Associate
Professor of
Romance Studies;
Associate Professor
of Art, Art History
& Visual Studies*

Thavolia Glymph
Professor of History

R. Darren Gobert
*William and Sue
Gross Professor of
Theater Studies*

Tsitsi Ella Jaji
*Associate Professor
of English*

Paul Jaskot
*Professor and
Department Chair
of Art, Art History &
Visual Studies*

Shambhavi Kaul
*Associate Professor
of the Practice of
Art, Art History &
Visual Studies*

Ranjana Khanna
*Professor
of Literature and
Director of the
Franklin Humanities
Institute*

Mark Anthony Neal
*James B. Duke
Distinguished
Professor of African
and African
American Studies*

Mark Olson
*Associate Professor
of the Practice of
Art, Art History &
Visual Studies*

Christine Payne
*Yoh Family
Associate Professor
of Mechanical
Engineering and
Materials Science*

Richard J. Powell
*John Spencer
Bassett Distinguished
Professor, Art,
Art History & Visual
Studies*

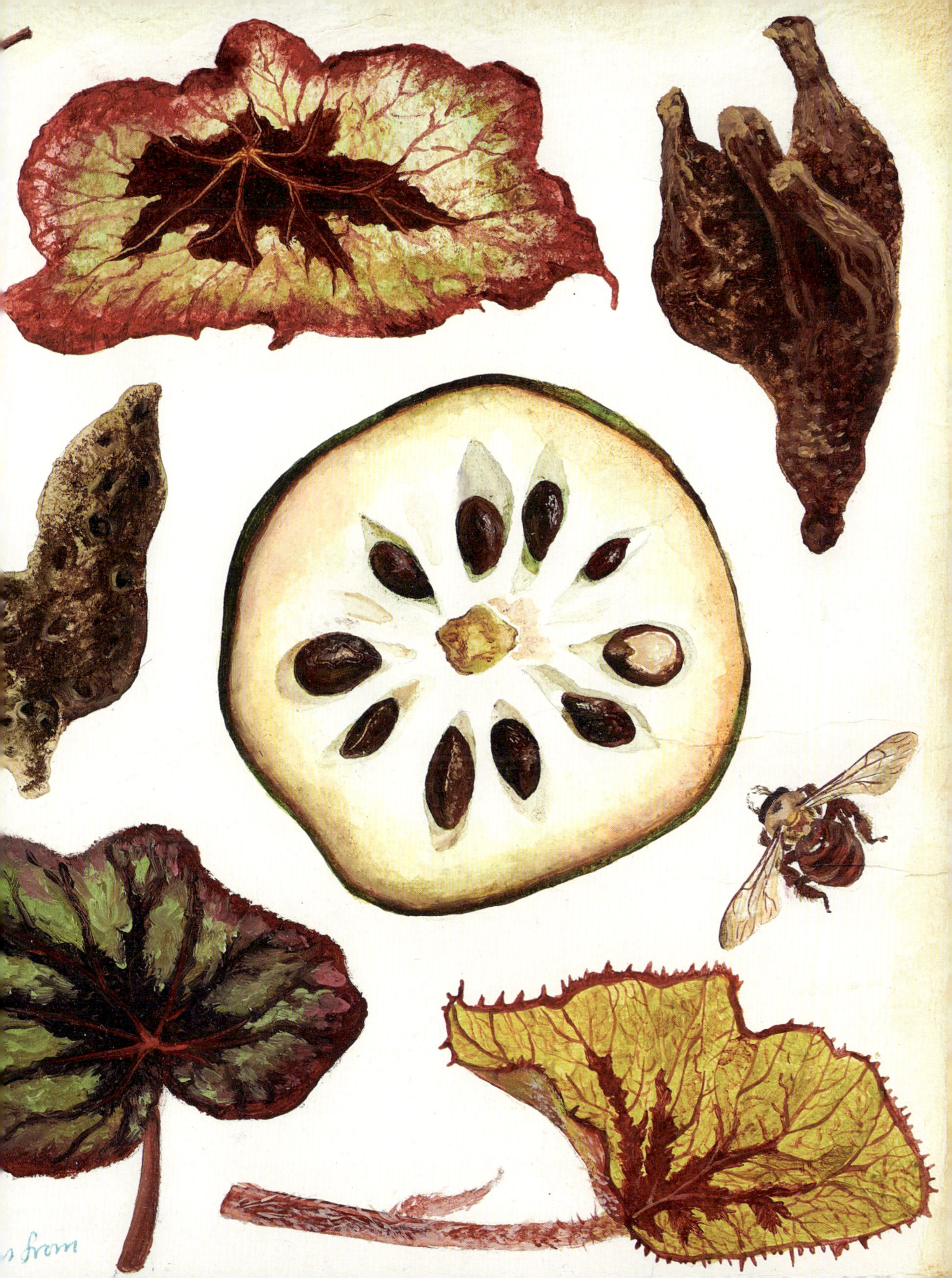

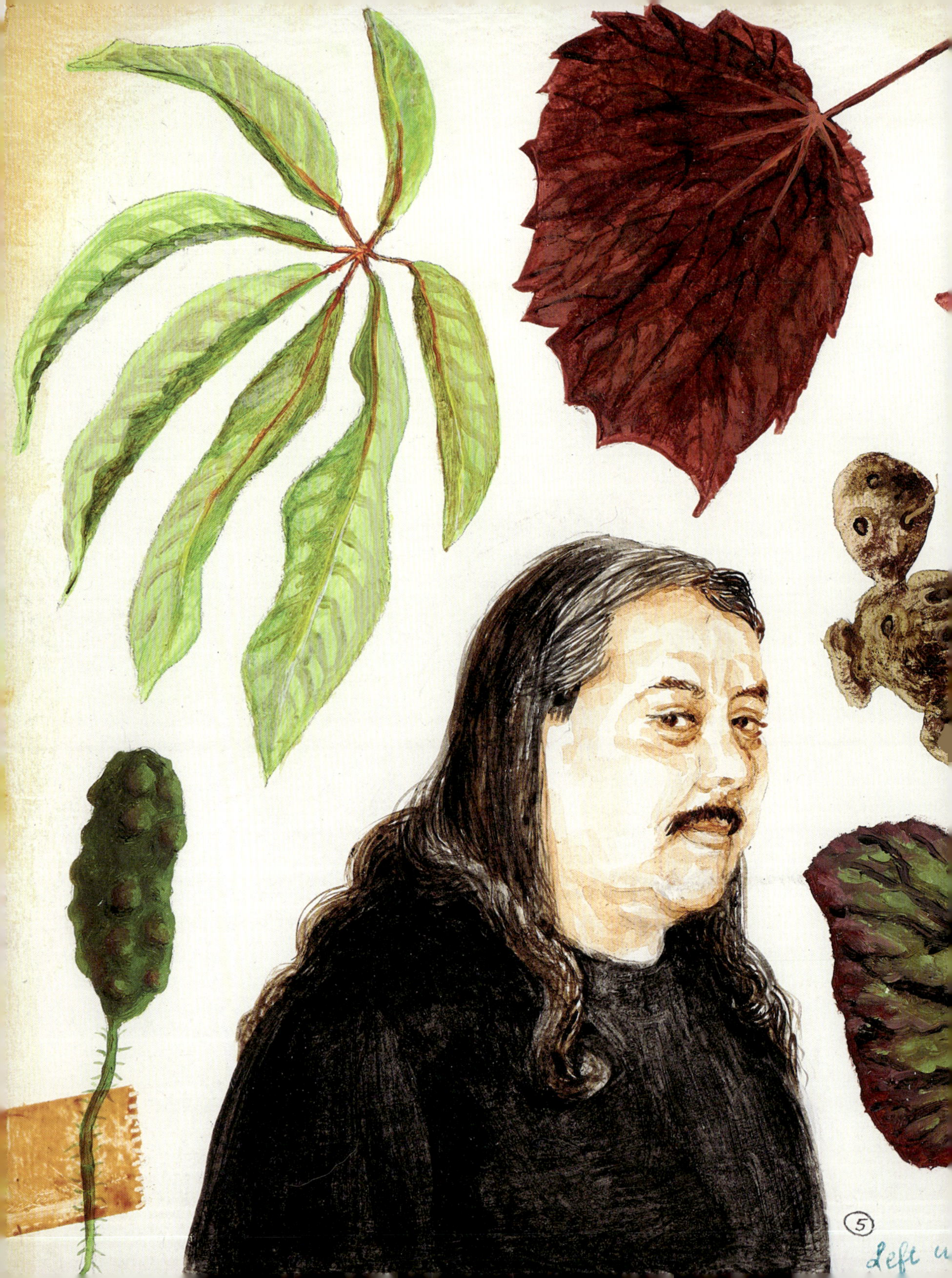

⑤
left u